Quick and Dirty

A Compact Guide to
Writing, Reading, and Research

FOURTH EDITION

Fred Cooksey

Crooked Pig Press

Easthampton, Massachusetts

CROOKED PIG PRESS

Easthampton, Massachusetts 01027

413.282.8701

For Zoe, Betsy, Mom, and Ramona

facebook.com/quickanddirty

CONTENTS

III RESEARCH AND DOCUMENTATION

Preface

Why is it called *Quick and Dirty*?

You don't hear it much anymore, but people used to say, "Just give me the quick and dirty." It meant: Tell me what I need to know efficiently and without excess explanation. That was my goal in writing this book—to give students the information they need about writing, reading, and research quickly, and in simple terms.

Acknowledgements

I would like to thank my many colleagues in the Holyoke Community College English Department who have used this book in their courses: Jennifer Abeles, Jane Burkhardt, Jackie Dailey, Lori Desrosiers, Michael Fournier, Sarah Gilleman, Jonathan Gould, Ben Hersey, Frank Johnson, Pat Kennedy, Christopher Kobylinsky, Naomi Lesley, Lida Lewis, Lisa Mahon, Don Matus, Petriana Monize, Dorothy Pam, Michael Roberts, Sean Reagan, Jonathan Ruseski, Elizabeth Trobaugh, Alex Wagman, Mike Walker, Sarah Willburn, and Carolyn Zaikowski. Their feedback has been essential to the continued improvement of this book.

I would also like to thank Alexandra Wagman for her extensive and insightful feedback on analytical writing; Sarah Gilleman for allowing me to share her work on thesis statements; Christopher Kobylinsky and Shelby Kreiger for their thorough and exacting attention to the new MLA guidelines; Kiersten Delfox-Conrad for her close attention to the APA student essay, as well as many other parts of the book; and Shira Simon, Naomi Lesley, and Meghan Baldwin Lau for proofreading.

Mere gratitude does not sufficiently express my appreciation for the patience and wisdom of my wife, Betsy Gillen, who has read and critiqued this book numerous times; I can always count on Betsy to identify and correct my lapses, errors, and misjudgments (in text as in life).

Finally, thanks to the many students who have offered kind words of encouragement as well as some very useful suggestions.

Fred Cooksey
August 2016

chapter 1

COLLEGE SURVIVAL
OR, WHAT *NOT* TO DO IN YOUR CLASSES

Only the educated are free.
> ~ Epictetus

The more we learn the more we realize how little we know.
> ~ R. Buckminster Fuller

What does a college degree mean in America today?

A piece of paper.

That's how students often talk about it, and that—in many ways—is how many employers view it.

Particularly in the world of work, a college degree means that you are able to complete a variety of time-consuming, sometimes demanding, and sometimes tedious tasks. Some of those tasks will require you to apply every ounce of your intelligence, while others will call only on your ability to memorize trivial information that you will probably forget within a matter of hours.

Finishing college may or may not make you smarter, but it will certainly prove that you have discipline. That's one reason employers want people with college degrees. When you complete a degree, it communicates to potential employers, "I am able to complete many tasks, even when some of them are not interesting to me personally."

That's an admirable personal quality, one that you will find useful in any number of real-life situations.

However. This is a big However. What I just described is what college "represents" in our world. That doesn't mean that college can't—and shouldn't—be much more. It *should* make you a deeper and more analytical thinker. It *should* expose you to new ideas that cause you to rethink your understanding of the world. It *should* allow you to approach intellectual and practical problems in more creative and productive ways. It *should* make you a better citizen.

As someone who believes in the ability of college to do all of those things (and more), I'm asking you to try to pursue those high-minded ideals. Avoid courses that ask you only to memorize and regurgitate information. Seek out courses that turn your intellectual world upside-down, that confuse and bewilder and challenge you.

It's worth it.

* * *

So here you are in college. Maybe you're eighteen and just out of high school. Or you took some time off (a year? twenty years?) to work, have a family. Whoever you are, if you're reading this, it's most likely because you're taking English composition (or "first-year writing," or "freshman comp"—whatever your college calls it).

It's the one course that nearly every college student in America must take, and one that many students dread. But it doesn't have to be that way. Much of that dread, I believe, comes from fear—fear of red "correction" marks (like blood) all over your papers, fear of assignments and directions you don't understand.

That fear is what motivated me to write this book. My goal was to create a brief guide to the most important skills you need to start writing at the college level. For me, that begins with survival skills. Plenty of books suggest "techniques for success," but I find most of the suggestions clichéd: study hard, don't put off assignments till the last minute, take a multivitamin, etc. Instead, I'll tell you what *not* to do. It takes the form of a Top 10 list.

WHAT NOT TO DO IN YOUR COLLEGE CLASSES

10. Ignore the syllabus

Some students, it would seem, never bother to read the syllabus. This is a big mistake, and one that will often hurt you in the course. I understand—it's annoying that every professor has different policies around absences, grading, phones, late papers, etc. But it's not so different from the real world, where one boss will be lenient and easy-going while another will be strict and demanding.

Do yourself a favor and read the syllabus closely. Your professor will be impressed if you're able to say, for example, "I know that if I turn the paper in Thursday, there will be a half-letter-grade penalty." He might even be impressed enough to grade your paper a little more generously.

9. Use email inappropriately

When you need to call or email your professor, think about the language and form you use. Far too many students send emails that look like this:

> hi, i'm in your english class and can't come to school today my mom's car is in the shop and there are no buses around here so let me know what i need to do.

Even if your professor wants you to call her by her first name, you should try to make your language and tone relatively formal. It should not read like a text to one of your friends.

> Dear Professor _____,
>
> I'm in your MWF 10-10:50 English class, and I am unable to come to school today. I will continue to read the essay that's assigned on the syllabus, but if there's anything else I should do, please let me know. Thank you very much.
>
> Sincerely,
>
> Joe Student

A few basic guidelines: Use capital letters, as you would in a paper for class. Write in complete sentences. Thank the person you're writing to. Include a "closing," e.g., Sincerely, or Kind regards, or Best. Proofread.

Take the same approach to phone messages. Speak clearly, say your phone number slowly, twice, and thank the person you're calling.

Finally, try not to bombard your professor with email. Many of us teach a hundred or more students, and if we have to respond to 20 or 30 student emails a day (a common occurrence for some professors), it amounts to a lot of time that we're not able to use for grading, finding new articles to teach, and so on.

8. Talk while professor is talking

Rude, disrespectful.

7. Come to class without book(s), paper, pen, etc.

Makes you look like you don't care. And maybe you don't. But that certainly won't reflect well on you when we're grading your papers, tests, etc. I could pretend that we grade everything "in a vacuum," which is to say without thinking about who you are as a person in the classroom. But that would be a lie. It's like anything else in life—you're always making an impression on the people around you. What will yours be?

6. Make excuses and/or fail to take responsibility

You'll find a whole range of humanity among your professors, but I think that most of us tend to be compassionate—at least up to a point. We want to believe you, for example, when you tell us your grandmother died and you had to go to her funeral, and we don't want to penalize your paper for lateness as a result.

But this type of scenario puts us in a difficult position. You could be lying (we've been lied to in the past, we know that much). If you are lying, then you're getting an unfair advantage over your classmates. If you're not lying to us, then probably you deserve a break.

But here's the problem—how do we know the difference? And what about students who are too shy or private to share this kind of information with us?

I often struggle with these questions, and I'm not perfectly consistent in how I deal with them. Sometimes I give students a break, sometimes I don't.

The lesson for you is this: If you have a legitimate emergency that affects your performance in a class, talk to your professor. She might not make any allowances for you, but many professors do want to know.

On the other hand, you don't need to tell your professor about every little thing that goes wrong in your life. We don't need to know that you got a flat tire on the way to school, or that your alarm clock is broken and you can't afford to buy a new one because you just spent all your money on a new tire, etc.

5. Pack up papers and books before class is over

Rude, rude, rude—both to the professor and your classmates. It's noisy and distracting. When you do this, you are communicating to all who can see or hear you, "I have declared this class to be finished."

Relax.

4. Come to class late / leave class early

I've been persuaded by my colleague Victor Katz, a professor of art history at my college, that lateness is a worse "crime" than simply missing class. (Most professors, by the way, do not share this view, but I find Victor's argument compelling.)

As Victor says, "Late has victims; absent does not." By this he means that when you're late (or you leave early), you interrupt class, which affects both your teacher's ability to teach and your classmates' ability to learn. It doesn't matter how quietly you come in or leave—it's distracting.

3. Ask the professor "Did I miss anything?" after an absence

Of course you missed something. You missed *class*, that time during which I attempt to teach you something *every single day*.

Rephrasing the question as "What did I miss?" is an improvement, but before you ask this, think about how you might avoid the question altogether. If the course syllabus includes a calendar of assignments, look there to see what you missed. You might also ask a classmate before or after the next class you attend; maybe you can borrow that person's notes.

If you still have questions, then go talk to the professor during office hours. But don't expect us to go over everything we did. We'll give you a brief summary of the subject(s) we covered, and then it's your responsibility to figure out how to learn that material. This is true even if you had an excellent reason for missing class. We simply can't recreate a 50- or 75-minute class for every student who's absent.

In short, try to be as self-reliant as you can. Your professors will be impressed when you can figure out the material you missed and keep up.

2. Skip required reading

More and more often, it seems, students are coming to class without having done assigned reading. Maybe you figure the professor will be "going over" that article or chapter, so there's no point in reading it in advance.

Here's the irony of this development. For the last twenty or so years, professors have been encouraged to lecture less and involve students in classroom discussions more. Many of us have moved in this direction, but now, when we try to have an actual discussion about a reading, it often falls flat because many students haven't done the reading.

In terms of being educated, there's nothing more important than reading. Not browsing, not checking *SparkNotes*, not googling a summary—just good old-fashioned reading.

1. Become disctracted / become a distraction

If you're using a phone or some other electronic device during class, you're not giving the professor—or your classmates—your full attention. I don't allow laptops in my classes, though I may have to rethink this prohibition at some point. I recognize that laptops can be beneficial in a variety of ways (note-taking, vocabulary, fact-checking, etc.), but I also know that many students aren't using them to augment what's going on in class; they're using them to *escape* what's going on in class. They're checking Instagram or Snapchat or their fantasy football leagues, shopping for shoes, applying for jobs. All fun and even useful things to do. But not during class, please.

Of course, some students will argue that if a class is boring, then what's the harm in escaping for a few minutes? But the harm is not to you—it's to me and your classmates, many of whom are aware of what you're doing and are distracted by it. This is particularly problematic with laptops because everyone behind you can see what's on your screen.

I love the Internet. I spend far too much time on it, and not much of it is well-spent, so I'm not judging you. But I am asking you to consider how your decision to entertain yourself during class may affect the people around you as well as your professor.

Even if your professor doesn't have a stated policy about phones or laptops, I would encourage you to try to be electronics-free during class. There's a lot to be said for the old-fashioned approach of taking hand-written notes and simply being fully *present* for your education.

chapter 2

READING AND CRITICAL THINKING

*Too often we give students answers to remember
rather than problems to solve.*

> ~ Roger Lewin

*All of us show bias when it comes to what information we take in. We typically
focus on anything that agrees with the outcome we want.*

> ~ Noreena Hertz

All writing is rhetorical. This is a popular saying among English teachers. What
it means is that writers are always trying to get the reader to see things their way.
I'm challenging you, in this chapter, to think about how writers make rhetorical
decisions that—they hope—will cause you to agree with the "world" they're
presenting in their writing.

In college, you'll be asked to read three basic types of writing: informative,
argumentative, and literary. The difference between informative and argumentative writing may seem obvious, but often it isn't—mainly because many writers
who are trying to get you to see things their way are good at presenting their
opinions as information or fact. So, even when you're reading an article or essay
that appears to be plainly informative, you should be aware of how the writer
may be "positioned" on a particular issue. In other words, she may have a stance
or point of view that she wants you to accept.

INFORMATIVE VS. ARGUMENTATIVE WRITING

Informative Writing

- Most textbooks
- Newspaper and magazine reportage: articles that present the news but don't
  comment on it

Argumentative Writing

- Editorial and opinion pages in newspapers

- "Elite" magazine articles and commentary

- Most nonfiction books (even those that rely largely on facts tend to be "positioned"; there are very few books that do nothing but present "facts"—almost all will also *interpret* the facts)

THE BLURRY LINE BETWEEN INFORMATION AND OPINION

Below are the headlines and first paragraphs of two articles that appeared the morning after the November 2012 presidential election. The *New York Times* is generally considered "left leaning," or more liberal (aligned with Democrats), so I've placed its excerpt on the left. The *Wall Street Journal* is generally considered "right leaning," or more conservative (aligned with Republicans), so it's on the right. Keep in mind that both of these articles appeared on the front pages of their respective newspapers; both are factual accounts of the election results, but each offers different facts. More importantly, the tone of each is quite different.

The Left: *New York Times*

Divided U.S. Gives Obama More Time

Barack Hussein Obama was re-elected president of the United States on Tuesday, overcoming powerful economic headwinds, a lock-step resistance to his agenda by Republicans in Congress and an unprecedented torrent of advertising as a divided nation voted to give him more time.

The Right: *Wall Street Journal*

Obama Wins a Second Term

President Barack Obama narrowly won re-election, overcoming public doubts about his performance on the economy—doubts that challenger Mitt Romney appeared well-positioned to exploit.

ANALYSIS

The headline: Note that the *Times* focuses on the idea of the country being divided. Also, the idea of Obama receiving "more time" suggests that he hasn't had enough time to correct the country's problems. By contrast, the *Journal's* headline is absolutely factual. It strikes me that the headline writer might have been thinking of that old grandmother saying, "If you can't say anything nice, don't say anything at all."

Narrowly: The *Times* says only that Obama was re-elected, whereas the *Journal* describes him as having won "narrowly." Interesting choice, one that depends on how you define a "narrow" victory.

Overcoming: It's quite a coincidence that both papers use the word *overcoming*, and because they use it so differently, it's the most revealing word here. In the case of the *Times*, the writers make it sound as if Obama had a lot to overcome, and that at least one key element of this was the "lock-step resistance" of Republicans in Congress. The writer is implying that Republicans unfairly opposed Obama's attempts to improve the economy, but Obama was able to prevail anyway. It makes Obama sound almost heroic, as if he had to battle an unfair opponent but still won. The *Journal*, on the other hand, highlights the "public doubts about his performance." This wording gives significant weight to these doubts and implies that they are reasonable. The fact that the word *doubts* is repeated adds to this impression.

Final thought: Be alert to the fact that what looks like mere information often has opinion embedded in it.

TYPES OF WRITERS

WHO ARE YOU READING?

You'll have an advantage in understanding what you read if you know more about some different types of writers—and what their differences mean for you as a reader.

For example, let's say you read this sentence in an online news site:

Eating cereal for breakfast is far healthier than eating nothing.

Fine, you think—that sounds reasonable. Your first instinct is to believe the statement. But who wrote it?

The author's name (I'm making this all up to illustrate a point) is Jason Yost. You've never heard of him.

Now, how would you feel about that piece of "information" if Jason Yost were

   a. a researcher in nutrition science at Yale University
   b. a stay-at-home dad who dropped out of college because his girlfriend got pregnant when they were 22
   c. the president of a company that owns five major cereal manufacturers

The answer makes a huge difference in how we interpret the information. This is primarily because of two factors: motivation and qualification.

Motivation

Both the Yale researcher and the stay-at-home dad might be motivated by the search for truth; both might desire to advance our understanding of nutrition.

But the company president is most likely motivated by the desire to sell more cereal. Whatever "the truth" might be, the company president is far more likely to manipulate it so that it serves his needs.

Qualification

Like many things in life, this is not an "either-or" question. Think of it instead as being on a continuum, like this:

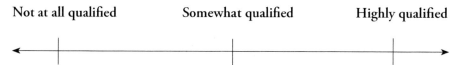

In our example, the Yale researcher is highly qualified, the stay-at-home dad is probably not at all qualified, and the company president—who knows? You'd have to find out about his credentials.

Sometimes it's not so simple to determine what kind of writer you're reading, so I'll describe some of the basic types you're likely to encounter. In case it's not confusing enough, keep in mind that not all writers fit neatly into these categories. For example, a writer might be a scholar when she publishes papers and books about marine biology—but when she publishes an opinion piece in the *New York Times*, she's both a scholar and an opinion writer.

REPORTERS / JOURNALISTS

Reporters typically work for newspapers and magazines. Generally, they are not specialists in any particular field—rather, they know how to gather information (usually via interviews, but also through primary sources like government documents) and put it together in a way that can be understood by a broad audience. It's also true, though, that at the best newspapers, most reporters are extremely knowledgeable about more specific areas: Congress, the automotive industry, education, etc.

OPINION WRITERS

This category includes people who write editorials, columns, and other opinion pieces. Their work can be found in newspapers, magazines and online publications (like *Slate*, *Salon*, and many others). Often—particularly at newspapers—these writers were once reporters.

When you read the works of opinion writers, it's important to distinguish between those who are "generalists" and those who are "experts." Most opinion writers are generalists—meaning that they typically write about a range of issues, none of which they are "expert" in. For example, a newspaper columnist might write an essay about global warming—and it might be quite well researched and persuasive—even though he or she never did formal academic work in environmental science, geology, or meteorology.

Sometimes, opinion writers *are* experts. Look for a biographical note about the author that explains who the person is; often this will state where the person works, which should reveal a lot. For example, a recent biographical note in the *New York Times* says: "John Farmer, a former attorney general of New Jersey and senior counsel to the 9/11 commission, teaches at Rutgers Law School." The writer, clearly, is an expert on law, which is the subject of his commentary. It doesn't mean he's right, of course—but it does mean that he should know matters of law that a generalist might not.

SCHOLARS

Scholars have been educated (usually through the PhD level) in a specific field, such as sociology, philosophy, English, physics, and so on. Furthermore, most PhD-level work is highly specialized, with the scholar focused largely on a particular part of his or her field. Within English, for example, that might mean eighteenth-century Russian poetry or post-war American fiction.

When you read a scholar writing in his or her field, you should expect to encounter a high level of language and perhaps some jargon specific to the field. There will likely be numerous references to other research done in the field, as well as footnotes and/or endnotes and a bibliography.

PROFESSIONAL WRITERS

That word *professional* might not be the best choice—but I want it to convey that the writer is an employee, typically of a large company or institution. Unlike a reporter, the professional writer's goal is not (necessarily) to tell the truth; instead, it's to depict the company or organization in the most flattering light. This doesn't necessarily mean that the writer is going to lie to you. But it's frequently the case that these writers stretch, twist, and manipulate facts so that the reader will be sympathetic to the company or organization.

Sometimes you'll find these writers in reputable publications such as the *New York Times* and other newspapers and magazines, many of which will include a biographical note such as, "John Smith is Chief Information Officer for Blandwood College," or "John Smith is the director of security for Giant Computer Systems."

When you see something like that, you should read the author with the understanding that John Smith's first allegiance is not to you, the reader, or to "the truth," but to the organization that pays his salary. When in doubt, do a quick Google search for the author to find out where he works.

CREATIVE WRITERS

These include poets, novelists, short story writers, and some essayists. Many have extensive formal education, while some have little. But we don't look to creative writers for "information"; rather, we read them to deepen our understanding of "the human condition."

TYPES OF PUBLICATIONS

Now that you know something about the basic types of writers you're likely to encounter, you should know something about the various publications you might find them in:

- The Internet (I'm leaving this broad purposefully)
- Online news sites
- "Popular" (or general-interest) magazines
- Daily newspapers (including online versions)
- "Elite" magazines
- Scholarly journals

THE INTERNET

You know, of course, what the Internet is, but you should be aware of the great range of materials to be found there. In short, start to think about how you determine which sites are trustworthy and reliable—because many of them aren't. See Chapter 7: Internet Research for more information.

ONLINE NEWS SITES

Again, there's a wide range here, and you should pay attention to who's responsible for the material you're reading. For example, if you find a news story on msn. com, it most likely comes from AP (the Associated Press, generally a trustworthy source of information). But often when you click on a link, you're taken to a "story" that is produced by a smaller, less reliable organization. Occasionally you'll be taken to an advertisement rather than an actual news story.

Basic advice: If the link takes you to a story by AP, Reuters, or a major daily newspaper, it's probably at least somewhat reliable.

"POPULAR" AND/OR GENERAL INTEREST MAGAZINES

What I call popular, or general-interest, magazines are those that have large circulations and are read by a wide range of people. As with newspapers, most of the articles in these magazines are written by reporters. But you will also find plenty of opinion writing—so you need to be able to tell the two apart.

If you're considering using popular magazines such as *Time*, *Newsweek* and *U.S. News & World Report* as sources for a paper, be aware that they are not highly respected in the academic world. As background information to help you understand the basics of a topic that is unfamiliar to you, these magazines are fine. But if you're looking for depth of analysis, you won't find it here.

DAILY NEWSPAPERS (INCLUDING ONLINE VERSIONS)

Newspapers have played an important role in our country's history, and in democracy in general. (The United States has the strongest protections for freedom of speech—and the press—in the world.)

In recent years, other forms of "journalism" have become popular. "Citizen journalism," for example, is an important trend; it involves ordinary people reporting on events in their communities. This reporting has great value, but be aware that citizen journalism does not always meet the standards of traditional news media.

When you read a newspaper (whether on paper or online), you must know if what you're reading is news or opinion. To do so, it helps to know the differences among the three major "parts" of a daily newspaper: news, editorial, and advertising.

News	Includes articles about recent events, trends, or people. (These should not contain opinions, but many media critics say that even "factual" articles tend to show the reporter's bias.)
Editorial	Includes editorials, opinion essays, and columns, usually about timely issues.
Advertising	Sells ads to individuals and companies. (This is how newspapers make money—which they've had a hard time doing over the last 15 or 20 years.)

Typically, those three departments remain totally separate from each other— you wouldn't want, for example, the advertising department to say to the news department, "Don't run that story on contaminated beef; we have $100,000 worth of beef advertising this month."

Something to think about . . .

The highest goals of journalism have traditionally been accuracy and objectivity. (Objectivity means that you're not influenced by your own biases.) Then some philosopher decided that "objectivity" was impossible, that no matter how objective we may strive to be, we will always be influenced by our biases, our particular intellectual and emotional history. The philosopher was probably right, but this idea has caused people—in my opinion, at least—to become unreasonably suspicious of journalists.

Yes, we detected clear differences in the *Times* and *Journal* coverage of the 2012 election earlier in the chapter, and this would seem to be proof that some journalists twist the news to fit their political agenda.

Still, I'd like to believe that most reporters simply try to report the news as factually and clearly as possible. In other words, with objectivity as their goal. Just because it's philosophically impossible doesn't mean that reporters don't still strive for it. And ultimately, it's our job as readers to be

TIP **Read analytically.** When you're reading a book or magazine and you're about to turn the page, guess what the word or phrase on the next page will be. After you turn the page, compare what you predicted to what the writer actually wrote. What's different, and why? On the next page, for example, what do you think the next words will be after "it's our job as readers to be . . ."?

alert to the ways in which writers try to shape (some would say *manipulate*) our understanding of the world.

"ELITE" MAGAZINES

"Elite" is a category I created because I believe these sources differ in important ways from popular magazines.

First, though, the similarities; like popular magazines, the elites

- can be found (generally) in mainstream bookstores
- are for-profit, with their main source of revenue from advertising
- are published weekly, bi-weekly, or monthly

Now, the differences are important, and they have to do mainly with the way the elites cover the news and issues of the day. Elite publications

- print longer articles that go into far more depth
- cover issues that are more complex and less focused on entertainment
- use language that is more sophisticated

Here are some of the magazines that I would include in this group:

The New Yorker   *The New York Times Magazine**
The Atlantic   *The Economist*
Harper's Magazine   *The Nation*

While these publications do not have the same standing as scholarly journals, they are widely respected.

* Yes, the *New York Times Magazine* is part of a newspaper, but the articles and essays published in it tend to be more like those in the other elite magazines.

TIP **Pay attention to the first and last paragraphs.** Most essays will reveal their purpose in the first paragraph or two, and often return to it in the final paragraph. Note: Some essays will begin by telling a story or doing something slightly unconventional, but in these cases the paragraphs that follow will state the purpose more clearly.

SCHOLARLY JOURNALS

No matter what field you're in, you're going to have to read scholarly journals, so you should understand something about why they're so important to the academic world. First, though, here's how they're different from magazines (both popular and elite):

- Almost all are published by a college or university.
- Most do not accept advertising.
- Articles tend to be less timely than those in magazines and newspapers.
- Few include images or photographs.
- All of the writing is done by scholars in the field.
- The audience is other scholars in the field.
- Many of the articles use language and/or jargon specific to the field.

What this means is that journal articles will typically be challenging to read, particularly early in your college experience.

Only one other piece of information is important to know about journals before you start using them, and that is that they fall into two categories, those that are peer-reviewed and those that are not. Peer-reviewed journals are the most trusted and reliable sources available. "Peer-reviewed" means that experts in the field (for example, leading scholars of abnormal psychology for the *Journal of Abnormal Psychology*) read and review all articles before they are published. These reviewers tend to be extremely picky about how arguments are constructed, how evidence is presented, and so on. As a result, peer-reviewed journal articles are some of the most trustworthy sources you can find.

This is not to say that their content will be absolutely *true*. It only means that they shouldn't contain any blatant errors or misrepresentations of fact.

TIP **Ethos, pathos, and logos:** These are the three ways in which Aristotle claimed that speakers persuade their audience. They apply equally well to writing, and you should be aware of how they operate on you as a reader. *Ethos* is an "ethical" appeal to the reader; it means that the writer is presenting herself as trustworthy and believable: "I have a degree from Yale, and my research has been published in many scholarly journals, so you should trust me." *Pathos* is an emotional appeal, one that is meant to evoke feelings of sympathy from the reader: "The chimpanzee had a look of fear and panic in his eyes before the test began." *Logos* is a rational, logical appeal, one that depends on reason: "If scientists are prevented from conducting tests on animals, research into traumatic brain injuries will end."

WARNING: MIND GAMES AHEAD

Passive Voice

Mistakes were made.

> ~ Presidents Reagan, Bush (senior), Clinton, Bush (younger)

Passive is the opposite of active. Grammatically, this means that the writer switches the subject and the object in a sentence, which forces the verb to change:

> Active: The boy hit the ball.

> Passive: The ball was hit by the boy.

In active voice, the "true" subject (the boy) of the sentence is first, and it performs the action. This is the most common way of forming sentences in the English language. When you switch to passive voice, the meaning is exactly the same, at least in this example. But it's a less natural way for us to read the information. That's the main reason to avoid passive voice as a writer. (Note: I'm not saying you should never use passive voice—only that you should know that you're doing it, and do it for a good reason.)

Sometimes, writers use passive voice because it allows them to omit the "true" subject, the person or thing doing the action, as is the case in the quote above: "Mistakes were made." This statement has become famous—and something of a joke among people who follow politics and/or language—because it has been used by all of our recent presidents to avoid taking responsibility. It should make us ask, *By whom* were mistakes made? But often we don't.

In short, passive voice is not just a grammatical issue—it's also an *ethical* one; here's an example that's closer to your world:

> Passive: Tuition and fees at the college were raised.

> Active: The college's Board of Trustees raised tuition and fees.

In the passive voice, the sentence omits an important piece of information: *who* is responsible for the increase in tuition and fees. As a result, we don't know whom to blame—or maybe it never even occurs to us to wonder who's responsible for this. We simply accept it.

Pay attention to how politicians and businesses use language (particularly when they are doing something *to* us), and you'll see that they love the passive voice because it allows them to imply that things simply happen, and that no one has caused them to happen.

EVASIVE LANGUAGE: THE ETHICS OF COMMUNICATION

In the example below, you can certainly figure out what's being said. But it takes some effort. The companies that write this "legalese" are counting on you being lazy—they don't want to make it easy for you to understand how to cancel your cable service.

A cable TV company

Original

Refunds/Credits will be given only when request for cancellation of service is received by Charter within 45 days of installation of service (30 days subscribing to the service, plus 15 day grace period for formal requests of refund/credit). Only 30 days of service will be refunded or credited.

Translation

We will only give you a refund or credit if you cancel your Charter service within 45 days of installation (30 days after you subscribed, plus a 15 day grace period). We will only refund or credit 30 days of service.

The original above is clumsy and misleading mainly due to the use of nominalizations—words that could have been verbs but are turned into nouns. Above, the first words (purchase and refunds/credits) are nominalizations. Academic writers and lawyers seem to love nominalizations too, but this appears to be changing—many editors and legal experts are now demanding clearer, more direct language. See the end of Chapter 5 for a more thorough explanation.

The lesson

Be alert to the complex ways in which writers try to manipulate you. It will help you become a better student—and a better citizen.

chapter 3

WRITING AS PROCESS

The work will teach you how to do it.

~ Estonian Proverb

Experienced writers know that "writing" is never as simple as typing up some ideas, turning them into sentences and paragraphs, and then running spell-check.

This chapter offers some advice about the writing process, but it's worth remembering that good writers rarely follow these steps exactly as I outline them. Instead, they tend to write in a way that has been described as *recursive*—meaning, roughly, that they go both forward and backward. They might go from brainstorming to drafting and back to brainstorming. Then, they might choose to revise a small portion of their writing so that it says exactly what they want it to, then go back to drafting again.

 Every day we read the work of professional writers in newspapers, magazines, and books. Because we only see the finished product—the thing that has been revised and edited (often numerous times)—we might think that the writer simply sat down and typed it. I can assure you that this is almost never the case. Even the most gifted writers have to revise. In most cases, the finished product that we read has little in common with the writer's first draft. Certainly, writing comes more naturally to some people than others. But even for those people, writing is rarely easy, and it almost never comes without effort.

Here's the basic process, in the order I'll discuss it in this chapter:

1. Find and narrow your topic
2. Brainstorm / prewrite
4. Create a thesis / determine your purpose
5. Make an outline
6. Write a draft
7. Revise
8. Proofread

Note: I'm assuming that you've already done some reading and research to prepare for the writing.

FIND YOUR TOPIC

All of your college writing begins with some kind of assignment. Do yourself a favor and pay close attention to it. Make sure you know what's expected of you, and reread the assignment occasionally when you're in the process of writing the paper.

If your topic has been assigned to you, skip to brainstorming / prewriting.

Three Suggestions

- Think about which class sessions you found most interesting. Go back and look at your notes for controversial issues, important commentators on the subject, etc.

- Freewrite about the broad subject—write down anything that comes to mind, including your own memories, observations, personal experiences. The goal at this stage is merely to find a possible direction for your research, one that, ideally, you care about personally.

- Explore the subject in books, articles, or online (see Chapters 7, 8, & 9 for guidelines). Don't think of this as research yet; instead, think of it simply as a way of exploring the subject in order to find a workable topic. But do keep track of sources you find in case you want to come back to them later when you do have a topic.

NARROW YOUR TOPIC

Start with a basic principle: If people have written entire books about your topic, it's not narrow enough. Instead of writing about technology and education, for example, narrow it down to how technology is changing higher education—or, more narrowly still, how PowerPoint is overused in college classrooms.

One of my students recently began with the idea to write about veterans' issues and higher education. To help him narrow that topic, I asked him to talk about some of those issues. He mentioned a number of concerns, but the one that he seemed most interested in was the G.I. Bill (a government program that pays college expenses for those who served in the military a certain number of years). Even that was a bit too broad, so he eventually focused on the current overhaul of the bill, often called G.I. Bill 2.0, taking the position that the proposed revisions to the bill were unfair to veterans.

Some of the ideas for brainstorming on the next couple of pages can also help you narrow your topic.

BRAINSTORM / PREWRITE

The key to brainstorming is to learn how to outsmart your brain. (See "Your Brain as Obstacle" on page 23 for more on why this is necessary.) Two techniques— freewriting and clustering—are often helpful when you're trying to generate ideas or find direction for your writing.

CLUSTERING

This technique is good for people who are visual. It can be done on a piece of paper (the larger the better), but it is often most successful when done on a big board with many people contributing.

As with other forms of brainstorming, the key is to not limit the flow of ideas. Still, there's a little more critical thinking involved in clustering because it does depend on making logical connections among ideas.

Here's how it works. Start with any idea or topic—try to express it in a single word, or two words at most. For this example, I'll use *education*. (See next page.) Next, think of ways to divide that subject into many parts, aspects, or issues— maybe ask yourself some of the reporter's questions later in the chapter.

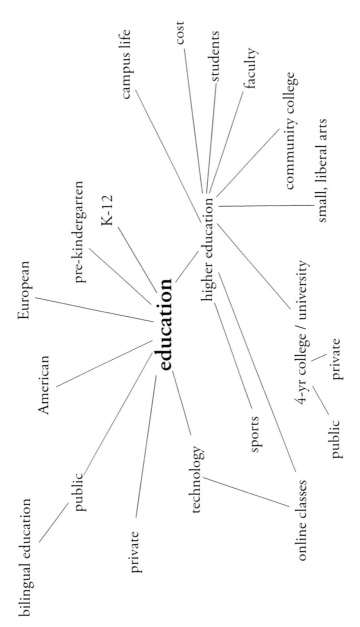

A couple of things to notice: If your "web" starts to move in one direction (as mine does toward higher education issues), you might start over with "higher education" in the middle and begin branching out again. Also, think about how pieces of this web could be connected. Combining technology, cost, and online classes, for example, could lead to a good topic about how these issues are changing college life.

FREEWRITING

One of the simplest ways to generate ideas for a paper is freewriting. The basic idea of freewriting is this: Write (or type—whichever you can do faster and most easily) quickly and without worrying about whether your ideas are good or whether they make sense. Don't worry about grammar. This isn't writing that you'll turn in—it's just a way to help you explore your interests, narrow your topic, and discover some possible questions about your topic.

What to do when you're freewriting

- Ask questions about your topic
- Try to connect different parts of the topic that interest you
- Answer some of the reporter's questions on the next page

What *not* to do when you're freewriting

- Worry about grammar or spelling
- Edit yourself
- Delete anything

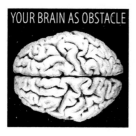
YOUR BRAIN AS OBSTACLE

Your brain is powerful—it stores memories, processes emotions, perceives the world, and reasons. It can be infinitely creative, but it can also be a source of self-criticism. Be aware of this latter tendency when you're at the beginning of the writing process; you need to allow your mind to roam freely without having your inner critic shut down ideas and possibilities.

Final thoughts on brainstorming

You'd be surprised how often something useful can come out of what seems like a bad idea. Some of the best ideas come after initially thinking, *That can't possibly work.*

Think about how creative many kids are—they invent games and "pretend" worlds all the time. Why? Because their imaginations are not limited by some "higher" voice telling them that their games are useless or poorly constructed. They just adapt the games, refine them, discard them, and so on. But they keep inventing.

Invention comes largely from a sense of play and often from lucky accidents. If you follow the rules all the time, the imaginative and inventive parts of your brain will never get a chance to function. And even though writing a paper for a class is not typically thought of as a creative act, there is still invention and creativity in the form of the kinds of connections (synthesis) you make.

REPORTER'S QUESTIONS

The reporter's five "W" questions (there's also an "H") can help you break a big topic down into smaller parts. These questions can also help you make connections among the parts. Here's an example of applying the reporter's questions to the topic of education:

Who	Students, professors, administrators, parents, school boards, legislators
What	Private vs. public, pre-Kindergarten, grade school, high school, higher education
When	Different time periods, such as 18th century, early 20th century, 1970s, the future, etc.
Where	Rural versus urban or suburban schools, American versus European or other geographic regions, traditional vs. online
Why	Origins of education: Why did education become "formalized"? Why do we have compulsory education? Why is a college degree so important to employers, or is this changing?
How	Methods of educating people: whole langue versus phonics, or lecture versus "student-centered" instruction

CREATE A THESIS

Once you have some direction for your paper, you should start working on a thesis. (This isn't always true—in some cases, it makes more sense to begin with questions and uncertainties and allow yourself to discover the thesis later.)

Topic vs. thesis   Your topic is what the paper is about; your thesis is what you have to say *about* the topic. It's your position, your stance. Readers can't disagree with you about your topic, but some should be able to disagree with you about your thesis.

Sample topic   Portable electronic devices (phones, laptops, etc.) in college classes

How would a reader disagree with that? He couldn't say, "That topic doesn't exist." Well, he could, but he'd be wrong; when you think of "the reader," you have to imagine a sane, rational person. So you have to add something to your topic that can give a reader something to disagree with:

Sample thesis   The presence of portable electronic devices in college classrooms has changed the way students and professors interact.

Not many people would argue with this, of course, but an argument against this assertion is possible. Therefore, it's an acceptable thesis statement. If your professor wants a more argumentative paper, your thesis could look like this:

The presence of portable electronic devices in college classrooms has adversely affected the way students and professors interact.

Keys to a good thesis
- take a position
- open up a discussion or continue a "conversation"
- be specific and sufficiently narrow

For example, let's say that you're in an anthropology class that's examining the many languages around the world that are in decline. You would not want a thesis that attempts to take on this very sizable topic. Instead, perhaps, examine a specific language that is considered "endangered," like Irish (or Gaelic, as it's also known). A more specific thesis statement might investigate whether funding for Irish language television programming is (or is not) merely slowing the inevitable death of the language. That would be sufficiently narrow and specific, and it would also continue a discussion that linguists, Irish people, government officials, and educators have had about the state of the language and what should be done to preserve it.

CREATIVE APPROACHES TO CREATING A THESIS

– COURTESY OF HCC ENGLISH PROFESSOR SARAH GILLEMAN

Take a biased position, add some evidence, then remove the bias.

Write a belief statement.	I've never liked Taylor Swift.
Add evidence.	I've never liked Taylor Swift because she pretends to be pro-girl, but her songs show young women acting petty, vain, and immature.
Eliminate "I."	Taylor Swift pretends to be pro-girl, but her songs show young women acting petty, vain, and immature.
Formalize the language.	Taylor Swift's songs appear to empower women, but her lyrics rely on outmoded, sexist stereotypes.

Refine or Limit a Thesis Using a "Filter"

Time	Taylor Swift's music is packaged as modern and original but is actually outdated in its depiction of insecure young women.
Cause	Taylor Swift's music sells because she embodies the cultural ideal of the child-woman.
Effect(s)	Taylor Swift's popularity has a damaging effect on young fans because although her lyrics rail against oppressive relationships, they do so in a childish, shallow voice.
Comparison	Katy Perry and Taylor Swift both claim to be feminist artists, but both singers represent young women as either luscious confections or avenging shrews.
Examples	Taylor Swift's songs appear to have feminist themes but in fact reinforce old-fashioned ideas about gender; her lyrics routinely convey outmoded, patriarchal assumptions about women's sexuality.
Problem Analysis Solution	If Taylor Swift wants to be an authentically feminist artist, she will have to write songs that don't fundamentally equate a woman's identity with her reputation.

PAUSE (AND DON'T FORGET TO READ)

You should know that the writing process rarely works as neatly as I'm attempting to lay it out here. Frequently, for example, you won't come up with a thesis statement until you've done some research or even drafted parts of your paper. The process of developing a thesis, creating an outline, and writing a draft tend to get jumbled together.

Depending on what type of writer/person you are, as well as the nature of the assignment and your familiarity with it, you should be prepared to move freely among these three tasks.

Most importantly, don't forget to read and re-read your source material. I sometimes see students working on papers without also looking at a book, handout, or article online. This is a big mistake. You should be constantly examining your sources and thinking about how to use them. See Chapter 6 for more on this.

DECIDE WHAT KIND OF PAPER YOU'RE WRITING

It might be useful to think of what your professors *don't* want: mere summary. Which is not to say that you don't need to summarize information from your sources—you do. (See Chapter 6.) But your paper needs to do more than just summarize a bunch of sources. All of your source material—whether summary, paraphrase, or quotation—must serve a purpose. Why are you writing the paper? What's your goal?

As you're developing your thesis and preparing to write a draft, you should also know what kind of paper you're writing. The most basic types of academic writing are informative, argumentative, and persuasive.

What you want to avoid is writing a paper that's merely a report. That might have been acceptable in some high school classes, but it's not what most of your college profesors will be looking for. There are some exceptions; in the sciences, for example, you may routinely be asked to write lab reports. These don't typically call for your interpretation or reflection—they want you to report on what you did and how you did it.

In English 101, as well as many other courses, you'll need to write more purposefully. To demonstrate, I'll use the topic of sleep deprivation.

If your thesis statement is, "This paper is about sleep deprivation," you're likely to have a paper that is little more than a report. If you want to explore the topic of sleep deprivation, you need to have a *purpose* for writing. Here are three ways to approach this topic with purpose.

Informative

Possible thesis statement: *Sleep deprivation has serious consequences for college students.*

An informative paper on this topic would likely examine the nature of sleep deprivation; it might include some history on human sleep patterns and consider competing perspectives (from science, social sciences, etc.) on *how* sleep deprivation can affect people, and how these effects might apply specifically to college students. It's important to note the difference between an informative paper and a mere report. An informative paper makes a claim which is then backed up with evidence and examples. It should also examine issues from a variety of perspectives.

Argumentative

Possible thesis statement: *Sleep deprivation can be a matter of life and death for doctors—and patients.*

This paper would share some explanatory elements with an informative paper, but the primary difference is that it would seek to convince the reader to accept the writer's conviction that sleep deprivation is an important issue in the health care system. It's argumentative because some readers may not agree that this is an important problem; their position might be, "Well, everyone would like to get more sleep; at least doctors make a lot of money." It's the writer's job, then, to convince the reader that this is a serious issue.

Persuasive

Possible thesis statement: *Local police departments should offer new scheduling options since sleep deprivation can be a matter of life and death for police officers.*

Again, this type of paper shares features with informative and argumentative papers. The key difference is that a persuasive paper asks the reader to adopt a specific position that could produce some change in the world.

*   *   *

You might be thinking: *This is easy, my audience is the professor.* In the practical sense, yes, you are writing *for* your professor. She might be the only one who will actually read the paper, and she's certainly the one who will be judging (grading) it.

WHO IS YOUR AUDIENCE?

Still, you'll almost certainly write better papers if you try to think of a real audience. Consider the example of the persuasive purpose on the previous page: Local police departments should offer new scheduling options since sleep deprivation can be a matter of life and death for police officers.

You may want to think about addressing the residents of your city/town. Of course, they don't have the power to change police schedules. But if enough of them call the police chief or the mayor because you've persuaded them that a change should be made, then you may get the outcome your paper calls for.

Thinking and writing analytically means putting yourself in the minds of the audience you're attempting to reach. One of the reasons we do research is because we can't always imagine the objections or questions our audience might have.

WORK FROM AN OUTLINE (OR NOT)

Some writers like to have a complete outline that breaks down every single element of the paper, and others feel far too constrained by such a plan. At some point in the writing process, though, it's generally smart to write at least a basic, informal outline.

AN INFORMAL OUTLINE

An outline doesn't have to be formal. It can be as simple as this:

1. Introduction, with thesis statement
2. Major point #1
3. Major point #2
4. Major point #3
5. Conclusion

That's the dreaded five-paragraph structure, which many teachers of writing despise. They say that it's too simplistic and limiting. I would argue, though, that many great pieces of writing use some version of this structure, and that most argumentative writing moves through at least two major points that prove the thesis. Also, the simplicity of the structure does not necessarily have to limit the complexity of your argument or the intelligence of your thinking.

The important lesson here is that your paper must have an introduction, a "body," and a conclusion. In the body of the paper, you must have separate distinct "parts"—these parts are generally paragraphs in shorter papers, but they may be sections in longer papers. In books, the "parts" are chapters and sections within chapters.

A FORMAL OUTLINE

If you're one of those hyper-organized people who has to have every last detail planned, this is for you. (Or maybe you should avoid it—because it might do you good to approach writing in a different way.)

A formal outline uses Roman numerals and letters. One of the most basic rules is that if you have a 1 (or an A), you must have a 2 (or a B).

I. Introduction—background: how education has changed in response to technology

   Thesis: Although many people are critical of online learning, it can be beneficial for all involved. (This is an acceptable "starter" thesis but would need to be refined in the actual paper.)

II. Advantages for the college
   A. Uses no classroom space
   B. Reduces maintanence costs
   C. Requires no additional parking lots

III. Advantages for faculty
   A. More efficient
   B. Convenient

IV. Advantages for students
   A. Convenient
      1. Better for busy students
         a. Some are parents
         b. Many work
      2. Easy for those with disabilities
   B. Less intimidating

Note: I've only expanded part of Section IV.

The subpoints (#1 and #2) give evidence for the larger point ("Convenient").

These points explain and/or illustrate the subpoint ("Better for busy students").

V. Conclusion

"I" STATEMENTS / FIRST PERSON: PROCEED WITH CAUTION

I think / I believe / It is my opinion / The point I am making is

Using the first person in an academic paper is a controversial issue, so I offer here a brief description of the two competing views. Check with your professor for guidance.

Many professors don't allow students to use first person ... for two reasons: first, they say that students who rely on "I think" (and its variants) tend to make personal claims rather than clearly reasoned points; second, many professors argue that the first person simply isn't necessary, as in this case:

> I believe that George Will's definition of reality television is too narrow, and that he ignores many compelling and worthwhile programs that use the "reality" format.

Simply eliminating the first person results in a more efficient sentence that doesn't lose any clarity:

> George Will's definition of reality television is too narrow, and he ignores many compelling and worthwhile programs that use the "reality" format.

But other professors ... are encouraging their students to use first person ("I") in some circumstances. They argue that it's good for you to use these constructions as a way of making clear—both for yourself as the writer and for your readers—what you are saying. Furthermore, using the "I" as I demonstrate below can help differentiate your ideas from those that come from your sources. For example, let's imagine that you've just paraphrased an assertion from one of your sources:

> George Will characterizes the emergence of reality television as the end of Western civilization.

In your next sentence, you want to challenge that idea. Using an "I" statement can alert your reader that he needs to shift gears and be ready to encounter your view:

> **I would argue**, however, that Will's definition of reality television is too narrow, and that he ignores many compelling and worthwhile programs that use the "reality" format.

(The transitional word *however* also helps the reader make the shift.)

WRITE A DRAFT

Many writers dislike the sight of a blank page. It can be intimidating, slightly overwhelming. If you have some prewriting and an outline, you have a real advantage. Either way, though, I suggest that you consider starting your draft not with the introduction, but with one of your body paragraphs. Many writers take this approach, with the reasoning that they can't really know how to introduce what they haven't yet written. The point is that there are no rules for drafting; you should jump around the parts of the paper as much as you want. Once you have all the parts in draft form, then you can worry about how they fit together.

Topic sentences

Like outlines, topic sentences often get no respect. They are viewed as overly simplistic, too obvious. Why should you say what the paragraph is going to be about in the first sentence so plainly? Shouldn't you just let the reader figure it out? No, you shouldn't. And there's nothing simplistic about a well-crafted topic sentence, one that lets the reader know what direction your new paragraph is headed in. Furthermore, even the most accomplished and respected writers use them, as in this example (a single paragraph, taken from the middle of a long article):

> But, as private colleges became more selective, public colleges became more accommodating. Proportionally, the growth in higher education since 1945 has been overwhelmingly in the public sector. In 1950, there were about 1.14 million students in public colleges and universities and about the same number in private ones. Today, public colleges enroll almost fifteen million students, private colleges fewer than six million.
>
> – Louis Menand, "Live and Learn," *The New Yorker*

The first sentence signals a clear purpose for that paragraph; everything that follows explains, clarifies, supports, and gives examples for the larger idea stated in the topic sentence. Notice also how the final sentence performs a "concluding" function for the paragraph as well.

Good topic sentences make it much easier for your reader to follow your thinking, but they also have an important function for you as the writer: they help ensure that *you* know what you're doing in every single paragraph of your essay. Writing a clear topic sentence forces you to decide what you're trying to accomplish in a given paragraph, and it might also help you eliminate (or move elsewhere) material that doesn't fit with the topic sentence.

Consider an example related to that topic of sleep deprivation. Let's imagine that one body paragraph will focus on how sleep deprivation affects the body. Here's a barely adequate topic sentence, one that would likely lead to a paragraph that feels more like a report:

> Sleep deprivation has many effects on the body.

Here's a better topic sentence, one that would connect to the informative thesis statement I discussed a few pages back ("Sleep deprivation has serious consequences for college students"):

> College students should be aware of how sleep deprivation may affect their bodies.

The next step is to consider what you do after that topic sentence, and this is where you need to know how to write *analytically.*

Analytical writing

Your professors will often say that they want you to write analytically, so what exactly does it mean to analyze something? Here's Google's definition:

> to examine methodically and in detail the constitution or structure of (something, especially information), typically for purposes of explanation and interpretation.

Let's return to the example of sleep deprivation and the topic sentences above. First, an example of the kind of writing that is *not* analytical:

NO Sleep deprivation has many effects on the body. It can cause "hallucinations, psychosis, and long-term memory impairment" (Maxon). One study at Harvard University says that sleep deprivation can lead to hypertension (O'Connor), which is also known as high blood pressure. Hypertension can lead to a number of heart problems, including "coronary artery disease, stroke, heart failure, peripheral vascular disease, vision loss, and chronic kidney disease" ("Hypertension").

That's not a terrible paragraph. It shows that the writer did some research and documented his sources properly—but it's mere information with no clear purpose. It offers the reader nothing more than disconnected facts.

It's also worth noting that the paragraph has no transitions, and this is often a good indication that the writer is not revealing how ideas connect to each other. (See pages 78-79 for more on transitions.)

By contrast, if we start with a broader purpose (for the entire paper) of illustrating how sleep deprivation is a problem for college students, a body paragraph of that paper might logically want to address the effects on the body. In this case, I decided to focus on a specific concern, namely, the possibility of gaining weight as a result of insufficient sleep. I decided to pursue this specific issue because I found quite a bit of research on this subject.

YES 1 Students who don't get enough sleep also risk gaining weight. 2 Most of the research suggests that this is because being sleep deprived can alter your eating patterns, often leading to overeating. 3 According to Chris Winter, a doctor who runs Charlottesville Neurology and Sleep Medicine, "If the brain is not getting the energy it needs from sleep it will often try to get it from food" (qtd. in Swalin). 4 A 2004 study revealed that one of the key culprits may be gherlin, the "hunger hormone"; subjects who had reduced sleep tended to experience an increase in gherlin, which the researchers determined was "likely to increase appetite, possibly explaining the increased BMI observed with short sleep duration" (Taheri et al.).

This paragraph could use more development and examples, but it should give you an idea how to use and interact with source material purposefully.

What makes it analytical?

1 Topic sentence

2 The second sentence summarizes findings from a number of different studies; this intellectual act is, by its nature, analytical because it involves synthesizing information.

3 The third sentence moves to a somewhat general assertion from a source that backs up the basic idea of the paragraph.

4 The fourth sentence moves to a possible explanation, one that is specific and which introduces us to a new term (gherlin).

What I've described above is a basic form of analytical writing. The next step is to *complicate* the information. By complicate I mean that you want to show some subtle differences in how your subject matter is being addressed by your sources. Primarily, this means looking for where they arrive at different explanations or interpretations of something.

Here's one way to follow up on the paragraph above while moving in a slightly different direction (this would likely be a new paragraph):

YES Other researchers believe that core problem is in the brain itself. Matthew P. Walker, a professor of psychology and neuroscience at the University of California, Berkeley, describes the effect of sleep deprivation as a "double hit" on the brain (qtd. in O'Connor). He notes that on reduced sleep, subjects were more susceptible to fatty foods and sweets, which "stimulated stronger responses in a part of the brain that helps govern the motivation to eat." This is the first of the two "hits," while the second is to the frontal cortex, the part of the brain associated with impulse control. In short, when we're sleep deprived, the brain desires foods that are bad for us, and we have less ability to control that desire.

Yes, all the information is from the same source—and in case you were wondering, it's not necessary to repeat "qtd. in O'Connor" because it's clear that I'm using the same source.

One last thought on this paragraph. The final sentence is a good example of purposeful restatement, which serves two purposes. For your reader, it helps clarify and simply some complex material. For your professor, especially in a writing course, it shows that you understand the nuances of your research.

ANTICIPATE THE OPPOSITION It might seem like a bad idea to introduce an idea that could contradict your argument, but it can actually make your position stronger. In fact, if you don't deal with obvious objections to your views, your readers often think of those objections, causing them to wonder if you're avoiding a complication because you don't know how to deal with it. Worse still, some readers might question your "ethos" (see page 16) if they conclude that certain complications haven't even occurred to you. In short, your credibility is at stake.

REVISE

First drafts are rarely very good. They are a starting point, little more. If you're lucky, you won't have to start over, but you shouldn't rule that out.

What I'm trying to persuade you to do here—for your own benefit—is change your attitude toward revision. If you see revision as the heart of the writing process (which it is, I and a thousand other writers promise you), you might be more willing to do the sometimes difficult work that is ahead of you.

After you finish a draft, you should at least be able to answer two questions:

- What is the purpose / thesis of the paper? (State it in one sentence.)
- What does each body paragraph do to help support or develop the thesis? (State each paragraph's purpose in a brief phrase.)

If you can do those things, it's probably time to let someone else read your paper—then ask that person the same questions.

If you or your reader can't answer those two key questions relatively easily, you have two options:

Option #1: Start over. It sounds awful, but it's often a more efficient use of your time. Sometimes, trying to fix a paper that has major problems (especially problems of purpose and clarity) takes more time than simply starting over. Professional writers do it all the time.

Option #2: Find what *does* work in your draft and start with this material; get rid of everything else.

MYTH: REVISION IS EASY

Revision does not mean to "fix" your draft. It's more than simply finding the errors and correcting them. The word itself, *revise*, has its roots in the idea of sight, and suggests "seeing again," or seeing your work in a new way. First and foremost, you want to rethink your ideas—how they connect, how you express them, and what, in the larger sense, they say about your topic.

Here's a simple but important concept my students often miss: If you're not sure what your paper is saying, or why it includes any particular piece of information or evidence, then your reader likely won't know either.

PROOFREAD

If you don't proofread your paper, it will most likely contain at least a couple of careless errors. For me, and for many other professors, a paper that seems to be the product of a lazy or careless writer is easy to give a low grade to.

Proofreading isn't particularly difficult—you're not concerned with the big ideas at this stage, just the correctness of words and sentences. You want the paper to feel polished and professional, so check for spelling errors, missing words, quotation marks turned the wrong direction, anything that might communicate sloppiness to your reader.

I have two specific suggestions that should help you find both careless errors and awkward sentences:

• Read your paper backwards, one sentence at a time (don't read each word backwards—that would be ridiculous). This forces you to focus on each sentence individually and can help you see your writing with fresh eyes.

• Read your paper out loud, or, even better, have someone read it out loud to you. Listen for places where the person has difficulty reading a sentence or finding the right rhythm—that's often a sign that a sentence needs to be rewritten.

TIP: USE THE CLOUD

Don't lose that file—save it to the cloud

I have computers at home and at work, and a laptop, and a phone. In the past, I had to be careful about working on a document—like this book—from one computer, then making sure I had saved that version (to a thumb drive) and moved it to my other computers. Now, thanks to the cloud, I can work on a file at home, give it a moment to sync, and then find the updated version on my two other computers and my phone.

I can also access all my files from any computer with Internet access.

Many sites offer cloud storage, but Dropbox is well established and strikes me as very secure. Still, you should take normal precautions with any personal information you store in the cloud.

SAMPLE STUDENT PAPER

This paper was written by a student in my English composition course a few years ago. I chose it because it has quality research, strong writing, and solid organization.

How to format your paper

Margins: 1 inch on all sides. Indent all paragraphs 1/2 inch, using either the Tab key or the Indent function (*Format* menu, *Paragraph*, then *Indentation).*

Spacing: Double-space all text. (After selecting all of your text, open the *Format* menu, select *Paragraph* and then *Line Spacing.*)

Specific formatting elements

1   Your last name and page number should appear on every page. See pages 40-41 for how to do it using a header.

2   Your name and class information should appear in the order shown here. Double-space this information just as you do the rest of the paper.

3   Title: Don't use bold, italics or underlining. Also, you generally don't use quotation marks, with one exception: if you use a quotation within your title, that part would need quotation marks. For example, if Kyle had wanted to use part of the quote from the bottom of page 4 in his title, it would look like this:

"Stand Behind a Register and Smile":

The Millennial Generation and Changes in the Workplace

Note: I think Kyle's title is better.

The Colon Is Key: A Brief Primer on the Art of Creating Strong Titles

The title of this box, like the title of Kyle's paper, exemplifies one of the basic guidelines for creating a good title—use a colon. There's a simple formula for the titles of many academic papers: start with something interesting and slightly mysterious, then follow it with a more conventional phrase or clause that clarifies what your paper is actually doing.

Something Creative and Intriguing:

Something Standard that Makes Clear What Your Paper Will Investigate

Kyle Wright   2

Professor Cooksey

English 101.29

6 December 2012

New Collar Workforce:

3

Catalysts for Progressive Change in the Workplace

As the Millennial generation, a cohort with dates of birth ranging

from the 1980s to early 2000, enters the workforce, analysis surrounding

this new generation attempts to uncover just what this digitally native,

feedback-driven demographic has to offer. As this demographic begins

to gain distinction from its predecessor Generation X, these young

people will have a significant impact on the modern workplace. Many

generational analysts insist that Millennials lack disciplinary traits needed

in the workplace. Professionalism, structure, and management skills

are common shortcomings of this demographic, according to a survey

conducted by Adecco, a human resources consulting firm (Bednarz). Of

course, it's true that many of the characteristics of Millennials clash with

the traditional work environment; however, the Millennial generation

will ultimately transform this outdated workplace into one that fosters

efficiency, productivity, and flexibility. Replacing expectations of

conventional structure and adherence to process, this modern take on the

workplace is one that promotes and properly utilizes this generation of

assertive and refined workers—a generation of born entrepreneurs.

Numbering in at around sixty million and representing ten to fifteen

percent of the workplace, Millennials are poised to be powerful drivers

Paper continues on page 42.

TIP: INSERTING YOUR NAME & PAGE NUMBER

MLA formatting requires that you put your last name and a page number at the top right of every page; here's how to do it.

1. Start by clicking on the **Insert** menu.

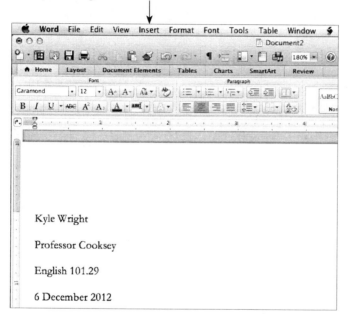

2. Select **Page Numbers**.

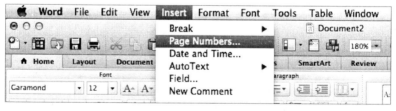

3. Select **Top of page** (**Header**), and **Right** for alignment. Then click OK.

4. Now you'll be in the header. Click here to right-justify.

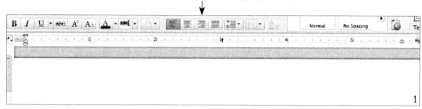

Note: If you don't have the right-justify button,
go to the **Format** menu and select **Paragraph**.
There, change **Alignment** to **Right**.

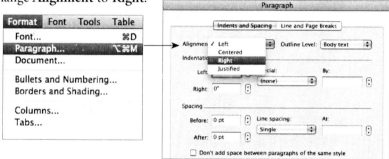

5. Type your last name, then
double-click anywhere below
the header line.

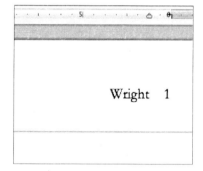

6. You're done, and it should look like this.

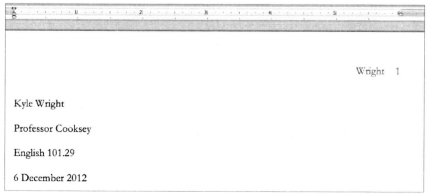

Wright 2

of the economy, both as employees and as consumers (Bannon et al.). Employers must work to meet the needs of Millennials entering the workplace, including flexibility, compensation, and opportunity. In turn, the characteristics of the Millennial generation will come to meet the needs of the business, redefining the workplace and creating a symbiotic relationship between employee and employer that will promote efficiency, results, and balance for both sides of the working relationship.

Stretching Our Legs: A Focus on Flexibility   4

In a recent study conducted by MTV, 79 percent of Millennials thought that they should be allowed to wear jeans to work, compared to only 60 percent of Baby Boomers (Kiisel). While dressing for comfort rather than professionalism may be an insignificant fashion change, it may indicate a much larger trend of freedom and flexibility in the workplace. Dan Schawbel, a Gen Y career expert and the founder of Millennial Branding, argues that this change toward a flexible and often casual work environment is caused by the Millennial generation's desire for a deeper work-life integration. Unlike previous generations, Millennials don't talk about balancing work and life, but rather about blending them.

Work-life balance is a growing concern for the Millennial generation, who refuse to work long hours at the expense of their personal life. According to the Pew Research Center, when asked to rate how important various life goals were to them, Millennials ranked being a good parent

4   Kyle uses section headings in this paper, which can help the reader see the organization of your paper more clearly—but they are no substitute for good transitions. Also, some professors may not want you to use section headings, so check first.

Wright 3

as a top priority, and the importance of the family outranked fame and fortune (Bannon et al.). Life goals such as parenting and spending time with the family may cause Millennials to challenge the conventional nine-to-five workday in favor of a flexible schedule that allows for better integration of their personal and professional lives (Bannon et al.). To create a balance between a productive career and a healthy lifestyle, the Millennial generation's redefined workplace emphasizes quality of work over number of hours and success over a structured adherence to schedule.

A few companies—Best Buy, I.B.M., and Capital One Financial   5
Corporation—have begun to embrace the Millennial desire for a healthy and flexible work-life balance in radical and exciting ways. Best Buy human resource managers Cali Ressler and Jody Thompson have developed the Results-Only Work Environment, or ROWE. This program offers employees complete control over their time, so long as their work gets done. As Ressler and Thompson explain in their book *Why Work Sucks and How to Fix It*, "A true ROWE has unlimited paid vacation time, no schedules, no mandatory meetings, and no judgments from co-workers and bosses about how employees spend their days" (61). Instead of rewarding employees on how many hours they log or how well they navigate office politics, ROWE advocates say that a relentless focus on results forces managers to be clear about expectations, allows employees to create a work life balance that is right for them, and increases productivity while reducing cost and employee turnover rates.

5   Note the uses of dashes to set off information that might have been confusing if Kyle had used commas, primarily because the three companies named here need commas between them. For more on dashes, see Chapter 5: Editing.

Wright 4

6   Even at Best Buy headquarters, however, ROWE isn't universally accepted. Tyler Shaw, a Best Buy employee and participant in the ROWE program, acknowledges, "There are some people who feel hostile about ROWE and want to continue micromanaging" (qtd. in Alsop 171). Managers voice concerns about this radical movement, perceiving it as an attempt by employees to get away with getting paid for "slacking off" (Barr). Telecommuting and working remotely have been around for years, but little evidence is available to show that these changes do much more than improve employee satisfaction and eliminate commutes (Weber). Shaw encourages his colleagues to look at ROWE from an economic perspective: "People spend their time like money, and time has power because it is a limited, nonrenewable resource. People spend their time in the most efficient manner possible to get the desired outcome." Through the implementation of a Results Only Work Environment, companies have boosted both economic results and employee morale. After migrating to a ROWE, departments at Best Buy reported productivity increases of 35 percent (Blakely). In addition, Best Buy's Strategic Sourcing and Procurement Team boosted employee retention by 27 percent, and saw a 50 percent increase in cost reductions over two years.

The Ambitious Generation

Raised in a world surrounded by breakthrough advancements—the boom of the internet, social media networks, and mobile computing—the

6   Note the excellent transition Kyle has created here. It works well because the first few words pick up on the ideas from the previous paragraph, and the word *however* lets you know that he's shifting into a different direction.

Wright 5

Millennial generation has become synonymous with ambition, a trait that defines a born entrepreneur. This ambition, and the many ways it benefits the symbiotic relationship between the business and the Millennial, is a dominant factor driving change in the redefined workplace.

7   While many Millennials are not driven to succeed by a fancy title or the corner office (Salzberg), this generation is interested in how their contribution to the workplace will make a positive difference. As John Spano, a human resources director for a movie theatre company, observes, "If you expect them to stand behind a register and smile, they're not going to do that unless you tell them why that's important and then recognize them for it" (qtd. in Twenge 217). Regardless of position or rank in   **8** the company hierarchy, Millennials' ambition will drive them to make suggestions to improve the work environment. Although this may seem disrespectful of authority, businesses should recognize these suggestions as contributions to the symbiotic relationship between employer and employee; managers should reciprocate by offering reasonable opportunity to pursue these ambitions "not by wearing a colorful T-shirt on a special project once a year, but [through] their actual work" (Salzberg). If   **9** managers properly utilize the ambition of this generation they can unleash

7   This sentence uses information from a source (Salzberg) in the first half of the sentence, but then offers a view that is clearly Kyle's in the second half of the sentence.

8   Kyle's source (Jean Twenge) was quoting her own source, John Spano; Kyle handles this complex documentation perfectly using the parenthetical reference and the "quoted in" construction to show where *he* read the information. See pages 143-44 for more information.

9   Note the use of square brackets here to indicate that Kyle has changed this word; for more on how/when to do this, see page 146.

Wright 6

the potential of "all that mobility and access to information" (Salzberg), and can build a diverse, networked, and transparent work environment.

10   Some argue, however, that the ambition of the Millennial generation does not always bring positive change to the workplace. As sociologist and Millennial critic Jean Twenge observes, "The optimism of youth, combined with the instant gratification that technology has provided, often leads to impatience" (219). Some young people will enter the workplace with unrealistic expectations of promotions, or see their career development process as a zigzagging line that allows them to jump around the company hierarchy at their leisure. "This is especially true of the most qualified young people," explains Twenge, "[who] have been encouraged to have lofty ideas about their future" (219). In this situation, both parties must be reasonable about basic expectations in the workplace. While a company may provide flexibility in terms of time management,

11 "employees control . . . how hard they work" (Alsop). If aiming for senior management positions, Millennials should be aware that they are going to have to work hard, often putting in long hours and travel. On the other hand, recruiters promising flexibility may mislead Millennials into believing they can work where and when they want from day one of an

10   Kyle provides a clear **topic sentence** for this paragraph; this sentence plainly states what Kyle will be doing now: exploring some complications to the argument he has been making. We call these competing voices **naysayers**. Using language like "Some argue" is an excellent way to force yourself to recognize competing perspectives.

11   Note the uses of the ellipses (. . .) here to indicate that Kyle has left out words from the quotation, which originally read, "employees control the throttle on how hard they work." See pages 146-47 for more information on when and why to use ellipsis marks.

Wright 7

entry-level position, when in reality these flexible options may only be available to a small group of experienced employees.

Looking Forward

12   In the coming years, due to the retirement of baby boomers and the relatively smaller size of Generation X, corporations will find Millennials to be in high demand in the job market. As the workplace changes, companies will need to consider how they "attract, retain, and leverage the future of our workforce" (Bannon et al.). Employers looking to unlock the potential of a generation of born entrepreneurs must work to embrace Millennial characteristics and utilize generational talents and skills. By creating a flexible work-life balance and harnessing the ambition that motivates this generation, businesses and Millennials can foster the symbiotic relationship that brings a fresh look and new energy to the working environment, while encouraging this generation of emerging leaders to continue driving positive change in the workplace.

12   Kyle's conclusion wraps up the paper nicely. Notice that he only uses one source here, which is appropriate—you want to make sure that *yours* is the dominant voice in the conclusion. The concluding sentences reveal his voice and his view on the subject, but these are not merely a restatement of the introduction; instead, he looks slightly beyond the scope of the current thinking on the subject to offer predictions about the future of Millennials in the workplace.

Note: Double space *all* lines.

Indentation:
First line of each entry: 1 inch
Second (and additional) line(s): 1.5 inches
See *Formatting a hanging indent*, page 179.

1 inch

1/2 inch

Wright 8

Works Cited

Adams, Susan. "Older Workers, There's Hope: Study Finds Employers

Like You Better Than Millennials." *Forbes*, 24 Sept. 2012, www.

forbes.com/sites/susanadams/2012/09/24/older-workers-

theres-hope-study-finds-employers-like-you-better-than-

millennials/#16b390cd4aa6.

Alsop, Ronald. *The Trophy Kids Grow Up: How the Millennial Generation

Is Shaking Up the Workplace.* Jossey-Bass, 2008.

Bannon, Shele, et al. "Understanding Millennials in the Workplace."

CPA Journal, vol. 81, no. 11, 2011, pp. 61-65. *Academic OneFile.*

Barr, Corbert. "Why Doesn't Everyone Work in a Results-Only

Work Environment (ROWE)?" *Think Traffic*, 31 May 2009,

corbettbarr.com/why-doesnt-everyone-work-in-a-results-only-work-

environment-rowe/.

Bednarz, Ann. "Hiring Preferences Favor Mature Workers over

Millennials: Study." *Network World*, 9 Oct. 2012, www.

networkworld.com/article/2160554/infrastructure-management/

hiring-preferences-favor-mature-workers-over-millennials--study.

html.

Blakely, Lindsay. "What Is a Results-Only Work Environment?" *CBS

News*, 25 Sept. 2008, www.cbsnews.com/8301-505125_162-

51237128/what-is-a-results-only-work-environment.

Conning, Denise, and Devika Cook. "Bridging the Generational Divide

in the PACU." *The Dissector: Journal of the Perioperative Nurses*

Please see Chapter 10 for in-depth coverage of MLA documentation.

Wright 9

College of the New Zealand Nurses Organization, vol. 40, no. 1, 2012,
pp. 27-36. *Academic OneFile.*

Kiisel, Ty. "Gimme, Gimme, Gimme—Millennials in the
Workplace." *Forbes,* 16 May 2012, www.forbes.com/sites/
tykiisel/2012/05/16/gimme-gimme-gimme-millennials-in-the-
workplace/#6edeaa071505

Miller, Matt. "Why You Should Be Hiring Millennials." *Forbes,* 3 July
2012, www.forbes.com/sites/mattmiller/2012/07/03/why-you-
should-be-hiring-millennials-infographic/#72ef8f4a37f8

Ressler, Cali, and Jody Thompson. *Why Work Sucks and How to Fix It:
The Results-Only Revolution.* Portfolio/Penguin, 2011. *Google Books,*
books.Google.com/books/about/Why_Work_Sucks_and_How_to_
Fix_It.html?id=dVK9ROrsDL0C.

Salzberg, Barry. "What Millennials Want Most: A Career That
Actually Matters." *Forbes,* 3 July 2012, www.forbes.com/sites/
forbesleadershipforum/2012/07/03/what-millennials-want-most-a-
career-that-actually-matters/#483301cf6dd8.

Twenge, Jean M. *Generation Me: Why Today's Young Americans Are More
Confident, Assertive, Entitled—and More Miserable Than Ever Before.*
Free Press, 2006.

Weber, Jonathan. "Why Telecommuting Doesn't Work."
Management 101, 6 Sept. 2009, http://business.nbcnews.com/_
news/2009/06/09/2912353-why-telecommuting-doesnt-work.

A WRITER TALKS ABOUT WRITING

CANDACE CLEMENT

Writer, Activist, Musician

Photo by Seth Jackson

Candace was my student at HCC for two years, and she was also the editor of the campus newspaper (I was the faculty adviser). We eventually became friends, and now, almost ten years after she left HCC, I still see her often.

After transferring to Smith College to major in American studies, she was pushed in new ways as a writer. She graduated cum laude eight years ago, and this interview was done during her final year at Smith.

Candace now works full-time for Free Press, a non-profit organization devoted to media reform. She also sings and plays guitar in my favorite local band, Bunny's A Swine.

Oh, and now she's a mom to Sophie.

Tell me about how you start writing a paper.

I don't know what the thesis is going to be so I have to read about it [the subject] before I can figure that out. And then I have to start writing before I know what I think about it. I feel like I make a jump from reading to writing, and that's when I'm really thinking. I'm thinking as I'm writing. 'Cause I write, like, crazy shit. I swear, I write half sentences. I'll write furiously for ten minutes about something, and then it'll just stop. I'll run out of steam. And maybe four or five sentences out of that actually end up in the paper, but I'm like, oh, okay, that's what I think of this.

I'm really bad at writing first drafts. The first draft is very stream-of-consciousness. I don't hesitate, I don't block anything.

You're not writing for an audience then. It's just for yourself.

Exactly. And sometimes, if I'm struggling with that, I'll try to write it to someone I know, like a friend of mine. "So, Tessa." She's my best friend. "This is what I'm thinking about this." And it'll help me because sometimes it gets too abstract in that stream-of-consciousness state. The first draft really is that stream-of-consciousness craziness, swearing, throwing in whatever, not finishing sentences. In the second draft I'll try to take that and write it to someone else, like Tessa.

Do you ever actually send it to her? In e-mail or something?

No, I've never done that. It's not always her, but I try to make it more verbal. So I'm not worrying about word choice and verb placement. I'll write the word *like*, I'll write the word *whatever*. I'll write *and stuff.* Because it just helps move the stream of thought or whatever along.

For the first few years of college, I would never do drafts of any sort. I wouldn't think I was doing drafts. But I was. I would write something, hit *save*, walk away and come back later. Now, there's more of a draft that happens, because I'll print something when I hit a dead end and I'll cut it up and I'll start rearranging it. Maybe I'll even split paragraphs. I'm big on short paragraphs when I'm in that process. If there's a cohesive thought that needs its own separate thing, it's in its own paragraph. And then I'll later join them and fuse them as necessary.

I'll play with the order of it. Then I write the transitions in and out of each paragraph. Unless there are two paragraphs that really need to go in a linear fashion, I'll save the first and last sentence of each paragraph to write much later in the process.

Sounds smart.

I think that's one of the things that when people say, *This is good writing*, they mean that it transitions well. I'm not totally great at it. In fact, sometimes because I wait so long in the process, that suffers. Another thing—and this is kind of a side-note, but something I would really advocate for. It's the downside of waiting till the last minute. You *need* to walk away for several hours, if not 24 hours at a time. Not look at it, not think about it, and then read it again. And I'm really bad about doing that. The one thing you'll catch is stupid grammatical errors.

That's also why it's good to have another person read it, too. Which I'm also very bad at doing. I'm insecure about my argument. I'm not really insecure about my style. But my argument—by the time it's developed, I'm more protective of it, and I don't want to share that with anyone but the professor. But I miss so many stupid mistakes as a result of that.

You know, a week after I hand in a paper, I almost always go look at it again, and say, *I can't believe I handed this in, and I can't believe I got whatever grade I got.* Except for one professor [a notoriously tough grader at Smith], who wrote on one of my papers, "I look forward to you knowing more about history." Well [with hurt look on face], I look forward to that too, I guess.

chapter 4

COMMON ERRORS

This is just the sort of nonsense up with which I will not put.
~Winston Churchill

Winston Churchill, England's prime minister during World War II, was famous for his wit and his eloquence. I doubt he ever made many "mistakes" in language, but his concern for what grammarians call "correctness" didn't stop him from making fun of the sometimes absurd rules that grammarians create. In the quote above, he's cleverly ridiculing one of those slightly absurd rules, namely not to end a sentence with a preposition (*up*, in this case). Grammatical rules are intended to enhance clarity, but Churchill's sentence illustrates that blindly adhering to (some) grammatical rules can produce comical and ridiculous sentences.

Correctness is a complicated subject, one that we English teachers don't always agree on. And the rules change over time as people refuse to conform to them; a hundred or so years ago, for example, this was considered correct: "He forgat his book."

A more contemporary example: people have started to use the word *anxious* to mean *excited*, as in, *I am anxious to see the new restaurant.* But the word's traditional meaning has to do with worry and anxiety, not excited anticipation: *I am anxious about my test results.* Still, many people are unaware of the "real" meaning of the word and use it to convey excitement. Can we really say it's wrong if so many people use it that way? Eventually, the dictionary will most likely offer both definitions, to reflect how people are actually using the word.

In short, the "rules" are always in flux. But that doesn't change the fact that you should learn and follow them in your writing, particularly in academic and professional situations.

COMMONLY CONFUSED WORDS

4.1   accept / except

Please **accept** my gift of $14,000 so you can buy a car.

Any car is fine, **except** a purple one.

4.2   all right (not alright)

Even though you see it all the time, there is no such word as *alright*. It's all wrong, all the time. (Don't feel bad if you didn't know this—I was on my way to earning a second master's degree before I learned it.)

The man left the emergency room when he decided he felt **all right**.

Note: You should also know that *all right* is informal—you probably shouldn't use it in academic writing.

4.3   a lot (not alot)

A lot of people went to see the artist's video of David Beckham sleeping.

Alot is not correct—don't use it. Also, you should know that while it is correct, *a lot* is informal; in academic writing, it would be better to express a large number more precisely: More than 2,000 visitors saw the artist's video in the exhibition's first week.

4.4   a part / apart

He is **a part** of the oldest club on campus.

This usage, as two words, means that he *belongs* to the club.

Apart from her car insurance, she paid all her bills without her parents' help.

This usage, as one word, means that this one expense is *separate from* the others.

4.5 effect / affect

Effect is (almost always) a noun:

> Moving out of his parents' house had at least one positive **effect**: It forced him to get a job.

Affect is (almost always) a verb:

> Moving out of his parents' house negatively **affected** his bank statement.

A complication you will only rarely encounter: Effect can also be a verb. In that case, it means *to bring about, or to cause to occur.*

> The Board of Education hopes to **effect** change on a system-wide basis.

An additional complication you will encounter even less often: *Affect* can also be a noun, meaning emotional state; the pronunciation is different too, with the stress on the first syllable.

> The referee's pleasant **affect** prevented the players from yelling at him, even when he made a bad call.

4.6 imply / infer

Speakers and writers *imply* things:

> The speaker **implied** that college freshmen were irresponsible.

Listeners and readers *infer*—or come to a conclusion about something— based on what they hear and read.

> We **inferred** from the speaker's comments that he believed college freshmen to be irresponsible.

4.7 it's / its   never: *its'*

It's is a contraction (the apostrophe indicates that a letter has been "contracted," or taken away) and always means one of two things: *It is* or *It has.*

> It's been raining all day. (It has been raining all day.)

> It's going to be a long day. (It is going to be a long day.)

Its is always possessive:

> The dog wagged its tail.

(If you wrote *it's* by accident, the sentence would say: The dog wagged it is tail.) See pages 65–66 for possession rules.

4.8   lose / loose

Lose is a verb; *loose* is an adjective:

> If you keep playing like that, you're going to **lose** the game.

> When the bolts came **loose**, the wheel spun off the axle.

4.9   then / than

Then shows when something happened:

> We ate breakfast, and **then** we went hiking.

Than makes a comparison:

> Stewie's argument was more persuasive **than** Brian's.

4.10   there / their / they're

There shows location:

> He put the clothes over **there**.

Their shows possession ("ownership"):

> That is **their** house.

They're is a contraction of *they are*:

> **They're** not going to be home.

4.11 to / too

To is a preposition and an "infinitive":

I'm going **to** the game. He's planning **to** quit.

Too is an "intensifier":

He has **too** much rice. I was **too** tired to go.

4.12 who / which / that

Don't use *that* when you refer to people.

> **NO**   Those are the students **that** wrote the editorial.

> **YES**   Those are the students **who** wrote the editorial.

You can use *that* when you refer to inanimate objects:

Here are the papers **that** need to be revised.

Note: you can also use *which*, but most American grammarians recommend *that*. In the next sentence, however, which is the only correct choice:

The revised papers, **which** I've attached to this e-mail, are ready for your comments.

A simple guideline: If you have a construction like this and you're trying to decide between *that* and *which*, use *that* if there's no comma, and *which* if there is. See also page 56 or do a Google search for restrictive versus nonrestrictive clauses.)

4.13 Who's / whose

Who's is a contraction of *Who is*.

Who's the man with the crooked hat?

Whose is possessive; it shows that something belongs to someone or something.

That's the man **whose** hat is crooked.

4.14   would have / would've   never: *would of*

Writers make this mistake for a good reason—because they write what they hear, or what they say.

> His argument **would have** been more persuasive if he had included better evidence.

Note: In formal writing, it's best to avoid contractions. If the writing is informal, it might be acceptable to write *would've*.

4.15   you and I vs. you and me (and other related errors)

Whenever you hear "That's between she and I," the speaker has made a grammatical mistake, and it's one that you should learn how to avoid in your writing.

Grammar people call it an example of "hyper-correction," meaning that the person who says something like "between she and I" believes he's being extra conscientious, grammatically speaking. He remembers being corrected by English teachers when he said things like, "Me and Josh are going to the movie." The teacher would have said, sternly, "You mean, *Josh and I* are going to the movie." And the teacher would be right because *Josh and I* are a subject (they're doing something), not an object (having something done to them, or receiving an action). So if you said, "The teacher hates Josh and me," you'd be correct, because in that case *Josh and me* are objects—they are receiving the teacher's hatred (or what they imagine to be her hatred; she was probably just trying to help).

Let's look at some examples.

subject   object

> Sally loves Hank.

When you introduce another person being loved, that's when things get complicated—both in love and grammar. I should say, it gets complicated when the other person is a pronoun: **I / me** instead of Fred, **she / her** instead of Wanda, etc.

> Sally loves Hank and **(I or me?)**.

The trick is to mentally remove *Hank and*; then it's easy to see the right choice. Think of it this way: You'd never be tempted to say, *Sally loves I*, right? So why would you be tempted to say, *Sally loves Hank and I*?

YES Sally loves Hank and **me**.

Now let's change Hank to a pronoun too. Is it *he* or *him*? Same principle: You wouldn't say, *Sally loves he.* You'd say, *Sally loves him.* So:

YES Sally loves both him and me.

Believe it or not, that's correct. It should *not* be, *Sally loves both he and I.* Never ever ever. No matter how many times you hear people on TV say it—it's not right, and educated people know the difference.

Note: If you're bothered by how your sentence sounds when you write it correctly, consider changing things around. Instead of saying, Oliver sent an invitation to Betsy and me (*not* Betsy and I), you could reverse the order: *When Betsy and I received Oliver's invitation, we hoped we would be out of town that weekend.*

When you use a preposition (*between* in this example), the same rules apply:

THE IMPORTANCE OF SOUND

Sound does matter in language, both in writing and speaking; when the grammatically correct way of writing something results in a sentence that sounds wrong, try to rewrite it. Often this means changing a sequence of two or three sentences, rather than just a word or two.

NO That is between he and I.

YES That is between him and me.

4.16   your / you're

Your shows possession:

Your hat is crooked. **Your** beliefs are ridiculous.

The second example is abstract. See Abstract Possession later in this chapter.

You're is a contraction of you are:

If you don't leave now, **you're** going to be late.

COMMON SENTENCE ERRORS

Think of your paper as if it were a house. You, the writer, are like the architect who designs the house. (You're also the general contractor, the electrician, the painter, etc., but we'll keep the analogy simple for now.) When it comes to grammar, though, you're more like an engineer than an architect.

Engineers are the ones who decide if a house is going to work, structurally. When the architect designs a balcony that hangs thirty feet over the back wall of the house, it's the engineer who would say, "That's not going to work." The engineer is less concerned with how the house is going to look, and much more concerned with whether or not the it's going to stand up and keep everyone inside dry.

We're not talking about what would look interesting. We're talking about whether or not the thing "works" grammatically—because if you have a paper full of flawed sentences, it's like a house where the walls are in the wrong places, or built from the wrong materials. It might look like a house, but it won't be safe. Now apply that analogy to a paper with numerous sentence errors: It might look like a paper, but it won't really make a lot of sense, and it might even fail in its most basic mission—to communicate with a reader.

4.17   Run-on / comma splice

A run-on sentence has more than one complete thought in it; it becomes a run-on when you don't connect—or separate—those thoughts grammatically.

> Jim drove his car into a pile of snow he could not get the car back onto the road.

In that "sentence," there are two complete thoughts; the first one ends after snow. That's a pretty obvious error, and not one that many students would make. But this version of the same mistake is less obvious:

> Jim drove his car into a pile of snow **then** he could not get the car back onto the road.

This sounds better, but it's still a run-on, because **then** doesn't have the grammatical power to connect the two complete thoughts.

Note: A comma splice has essentially the same problem as a run-on, but it has a comma between the two complete thoughts—which still isn't enough to connect the parts:

> Jim drove his car into a pile of snow, he could not get the car back onto the road.

Run-ons and comma splices can be corrected in two basic ways—either by separating the complete thoughts (with a period or semicolon), or by connecting them (with a variety of methods).

Separating with a period—acceptable but often simplistic

> Jim drove his car into a pile of snow. He could not get the car back onto the road.

Connecting —a better solution

With a coordinating conjunction (comma *before* the conjunction):

> Jim drove his car into a pile of snow, **and** he could not get the car back onto the road.

With a dependent word:

> **After** Jim drove his car into a pile of snow, he could not get the car back onto the road.

Or with a dependent word, reversing the parts (and changing a pronoun):

> Jim could not get his car back onto the road **after** he drove it into a pile of snow.

Conjunctive Adverbs

accordingly, consequently, conversely, finally, furthermore, however, indeed, likewise, meanwhile, moreover, nevertheless, next, nonetheless, otherwise, similarly, still, subsequently, then, therefore, thus

Be careful with these; used incorrectly, they often lead to run-ons or comma splices. Conjunctive adverbs typically need to be used after a period or a semicolon and are usually followed by a comma.

> **NO** The car was completely stuck, however it did not appear to be damaged.

> **YES** The car was completely stuck; however, it did not appear to be damaged.

4.18   Fragment

A fragment is an incomplete sentence. It can happen for a variety of reasons, most often because you've made one part of the sentence dependent—without giving it another part that's independent to balance it, like this:

> When there is no more gas left and cheaper sources of fuel can't be found.

It's that first word, "when," that makes the sentence a fragment—because it's a dependent word in this case. Like most fragments, the sentence leaves the reader hanging, waiting for something else. The thing you're waiting for is the independent clause, the thing that will make the sentence complete:

When there is no more gas left and cheaper sources of fuel can't be found, more research will be devoted to alternative energies.

Common Dependent Words

because, when, even though, although, if, in order to, since, though, unless, until, whatever, whenever, whether, while, after, as, as if, before, even if

Fragments *can* be good

Fragments aren't always a mistake. Experienced writers use them for good effect—they can break up the rhythm of your sentences and provide emphasis, as in this example:

> Storing explicit memories and, equally important, forming connections between them requires strong mental concentration, amplified by repetition or by intense intellectual or emotional engagement. The sharper the attention, the sharper the memory. (193)
>
> ~ Nicholas Carr, *The Shallows: What the Internet Is Doing to Our Brains*

The second sentence is the fragment, of course (there's no verb). But it's effective here because the sentence that precedes it is long and complex. The simplicity of the second sentence provides a quick, accessible way of thinking about the complex information in the previous sentence.

Purposeful fragments can help balance long sentences and provide a quick punch of information. But use them sparingly—too many fragmented sentences (even when written intentionally) will look gimmicky, and they will lose the power to grab the reader's attention.

4.19 Subject-verb agreement

Subjects and verbs have to agree "in number":

NO The paper go into that drawer.

YES The paper goes into that drawer.

4.20   Compound subject (subject-verb agreement)

When you have a two-part subject joined by *and*, you need a plural verb:

The chair and the table **are** in the truck.

Some writers are thrown off by the fact that table (which is singular) is right next to the verb, which might make them choose *is* for the verb instead of *are*. But *are* is correct because chair and table, together, become plural.

When you have a two-part subject joined by *or*, you choose the verb based on the subject closest to the verb.

Singular

The plumber or his assistant **does** a final inspection of the work.

Plural

The plumber or his assistants **do** a final inspection of the work.

4.21   There is / There are (subject-verb agreement)

When you start a sentence with one of these constructions, you have to choose the right verb (*is* or *are*) based on whether the subject is singular or plural.

There *is* one way to get rid of fleas on your dog.

There *are* many ways your dog can get fleas.

In the first sentence, the subject is *way*, which is singular.

In the second sentence, the subject is *ways*, which is plural.

Note: Starting a sentence with *There is* or *There are* is weak—try to rewrite your sentence to avoid this construction. (See Chapter 5: Editing, especially page 74.)

4.22   –ing subject (subject-verb agreement)

When your subject is an –ing word (also called a *gerund*), you need a singular verb. (This error, by the way, appeared in the *New York Times*.)

Singular   Plural

NO The awarding of contracts to Pearson in Kentucky and Virginia illustrate the problem.

Singular   Singular

YES The awarding of contracts to Pearson in Kentucky and Virginia illustrates the problem.

4.23   Interruptions (subject-verb agreement)

In English, we tend to like the subject and verb right next to each other, but sometimes we want to separate them, as in this example:

> **NO** The drummer, but not any of the other musicians, have real talent.

> **YES** The drummer, but not any of the other musicians, has real talent.

Some writers might have been tempted to think that the plural noun *musicians* would make the next verb *have* instead of *has*. But if you remove the "interruption" (all of the information inside the two commas), it's easy to see that *the drummer* is the subject and that *has* is the right verb.

4.24   Pronoun reference errors

These errors usually occur when you have a singular (meaning one) subject that you mistakenly connect to a plural (more than one) pronoun.

Singular   Plural

> **NO** **Each student** must submit **their** financial aid form by Friday at 5 p.m.

Four possible solutions:

> **YES** Each student must submit his or her financial aid form by Friday at 5 p.m.

> **YES** Students must submit their financial aid forms by Friday at 5 p.m

> **YES** You must submit your financial aid form by Friday at 5 p.m.

> **YES** Financial aid forms must be submitted by Friday at 5 p.m.

Note: As is often the case in language, these rules are in flux. It's relatively common now to encounter people who don't want to identified by "gendered" pronouns. In other words, a person may appear female but not want to be identified as *she* or *her*. Frequently, the person will ask to be referred to as *they*. Like this: I saw

Sheila recently, and *they* had just started a new job. This construction causes strict grammarians some distress, but most people (even strict grammarians) would agree that it's important to honor a request not to attach a gendered pronoun to someone when he/she/they have made it clear they object. In short, what I identify as an "error" above might soon be deemed acceptable.

4.25   Faulty parallelism

Parallelism means that two or more elements are consistent with each other.

Parallel   Not parallel

NO The college's student government was responsible for **recruiting new members, submitting a budget**, and enforcement of all policies.

Not parallel

The first two responsibilities are parallel to each other, because they both begin with an -ing verb and then follow with a noun. The third responsibility, in order to be parallel, must also start with an -ing verb (enforcing) and follow with a noun.

YES The college's student government was responsible for **recruiting new members, submitting a budget**, and **enforcing all policies**.

Parallel

A FEW RULES WORTH LEARNING

I've always believed that English teachers rely too much on rules—and that students learn to write more clearly as a result of reading and practice. Still, you'll avoid a lot of mistakes if you refer to these guidelines for apostrophes, commas, titles, and capitalization.

Apostrophes for contractions

A contraction means that something becomes smaller. With words, contractions are formed with apostrophes: is not = isn't.

The apostrophe here shows that a letter has been removed. The principle is the same even if the apostrophe replaces more letters:

would have = would've

Note: Avoid contractions in formal academic writing.

Apostrophes for possession

When we speak, we create the "sound" of possession by adding an *s* sound. But when we write, we use an apostrophe.

I offer four rules for apostrophes here. If you learn the first two, you'll get the apostrophe right 70 percent of the time. Learn all four and you'll never make an apostrophe mistake.

Rule #1: Don't add apostrophes to words that are simply plurals.

In this example, some people would be tempted to put an apostrophe somewhere in the word *cars*.

Five cars were left in the parking lot overnight.

But nothing "belongs" to the cars here, so there's no apostrophe.

Rule #2: In most cases, just add 's to the word doing the possessing:

Here, the trunk "belongs to"—or is a part of—the car, so you add 's to car.

One car's trunk had been broken into.

Here, one cat "possesses" a paw:

The cat's paw got caught in the door.

The rule is the same if the person/animal/thing doing the possessing ends with the letter s; pretend that the cat is named James:

James's paw got caught in the door.

Also, it doesn't matter if the cat had managed to get two paws stuck in the door—the possession rule would be the same:

The cat's paws got caught in the door.

Okay, it probably matters to the cat, but it doesn't matter to us, at least not grammatically.

Rule #3: When more than one person or thing is doing the possessing, the apostrophe usually goes after the s.

In this example, *cars* is plural in the first sentence (so no apostrophe), but possessive in the second sentence (so it needs an apostrophe).

> Five cars were left in the parking lot overnight. All the cars' windshields were smashed.

Also remember that it wouldn't matter if we added an adjective: "the cars' *dirty* windshields."

Rule #4: Possession with plural words like men, women, etc.

The plural form of most words ends with an s: tables, chairs, elephants, houses, trees, and so on. But some words—like *women, people, men*—form a plural without the final s. When the plural form of a word does not end in s, add 's.

> The women's room is down the hall, on your left.

(The room that "belongs to" women is down the hall.)

ABSTRACT POSSESSION

Often, the idea of possession is obvious: Something "belongs" to someone: Jim's hat, or Tina's car. But there's another form of "possession" that is less obvious, mainly because it isn't physical. Think of it as abstract, or conceptual, possession. For example:

> Mike's anger caused him to lose his job.

Does Mike "possess" his anger? Not in any physical sense—but in a grammatical sense, yes. The most common form of abstract possession is emotional: Mike's anger, Tina's love of her children, Paul's fear of dogs, etc. But other types of possession are even harder to detect because they involve what I'll call an "abstract state of being."

> Mike's inability to control his anger caused him to lose his job.

Again, it's hard to think of "inability" as belonging to Mike, but it does.

Commas

Six rules cover just about every use of the comma. Here they are:

After introductory material

After the judge's recess, the plaintiff disappeared.

Nonetheless, all the cars were ticketed.

Around an "interruption"

James, the oldest boy in the class, was also the tallest.

With items in a list or series

The recipe calls for apples, pears, peaches, and cinnamon.

(Note: The comma after the next-to-last item in the list—*peaches*, in this case—is the subject of great controversy among grammar geeks. Some consider it optional, while others insist it must be included. If you're curious, Google *Oxford comma*.)

Between two complete thoughts, with a conjunction

The police officer arrested the student protesters, but a judge later ruled that the officer had used excessive force.

With many uses of *which* (aka nonrestrictive clauses)

Her favorite food was artichokes, which he found repulsive.

I explain the grammatical rule in the next few examples, but it may be just as helpful for you to simply listen for the slight pause that usually occurs in these constructions.

When to use *that* versus *which* can be confusing, particularly when you're trying to determine whether or not you need a comma; grammatically, the key is to know whether you're dealing with a restrictive or a nonrestrictive clause:

Cell phones that ring during movies are extremely annoying.

Here, the meaning of cell phones is *restricted*—the sentence says that in *one specific circumstance* (during a movie) cell phones are annoying. No comma is needed.

Cell phones, which became widely available in the mid-90s, can be extremely useful.

Here, the meaning is *not* restricted—the sentence says that cell phones can be extremely useful. The other piece of information is not essential to the meaning of the sentence. (Yes, this example is very similar to the "interruption" rule.)

With quotations (see also Chapter 7)

Red Barber once said, "Baseball is dull only to dull minds."

Note: If the quote flows grammatically within the sentence, then the comma is usually omitted:

Red Barber once described baseball as being dull "only to dull minds."

Titles

Generally, titles of shorter works go inside quotation marks; titles of longer works are italicized.

Quotation marks

Article in a newspaper, magazine, or academic journal:

David Carr's "A Guide to Smartphone Manners"

Essay in a book: Gerald Graff's "Hidden Intellectualism"

Short story: Alice Munro's "Boys and Girls"

Poem: Seamus Heaney's "Digging"

Episode of a TV show: "The Red Wedding" (episode of *Game of Thrones*)

Song: Sex Pistols' "Anarchy in the U.K."

Italics

Book: Herman Melville's *Moby-Dick*

Collection of essays, stories, or poems:

> Seamus Heaney's *Collected Poems:1965-1975*

Textbook: *Quick and Dirty: A Compact Guide to Writing, Reading, and Research*

Album: Neutral Milk Hotel's *In the Aeroplane Over the Sea*

Movie: *Lost in Translation*

Television show: *BoJack Horseman*

Complication: Sometimes, particularly with poets, fiction writers, and essayists, the name of a book will also be the name of a story, poem, or essay within the book. For example, Seamus Heaney's first collection of poems was called *Death of a Naturalist*. So, when referring to the book as a whole, I would italicize the title. However, there's also a poem by the same name in the book; when I refer to that poem, I would use quotes: "Death of a Naturalist."

The title of *your* paper

Capitalize every word in your title except for the following:

> articles: a, an, the
>
> prepositions (even long ones): of, on, to, for, with, about, through (and many others)
>
> conjunctions: and, but, or, so, yet, nor, for
>
> infinitive: to

Example:

An Analysis of Symbiotic Relationships among Birds, Bees, and Flies

Generally, you capitalize all the "important" words. Note that *among* is not capitalized because it's a preposition.

Also, when you put a title on your own paper, don't do anything to it— no quotation marks, no italics, no bold. Nothing. The only exception to this is if you have a quote within your title, like this:

Landscape, Memory, and Myth in Heaney's "Personal Helicon"

Capitalization

People's names

Ernest Hemingway, Homer J. Simpson

Places

Paris, France; Wheeling, West Virginia; North Carolina's Outer Banks

Complication: Some "places" don't get capitalized: southern Virginia (because there is no place by that name), western Massachusetts

However, you do capitalize regions in some cases (but not compass directions):

Many people died when the West was settled. (Region.)

Chicopee is west of Worcester. (Compass direction.)

Languages / people / cuisines

English, French, Chinese, Russian, Portuguese, etc.

Organizations / institutions

Congress, the Department of Labor, Seattle Central Community College, United Auto Workers (because it's the formal name of a union)

Brand names

Kleenex, Apple (the computer), Panasonic, Tide (laundry detergent)

Professional titles / academic titles

Typically, if someone's title comes before his or her name, you capitalize it; if it comes after, you don't:

I met with Vice President Bausch for almost an hour last week.

The meeting was led by Robert Bausch, a vice president at the college.

Additional resources

To learn more about grammar and other issues of correctness, I recommend the site at Purdue University; do a Google search for *owl purdue grammar*.

chapter 5

EDITING

*The difference between the right word and the almost right word
is the difference between lightning and the lightning bug.*
> ~ Mark Twain

I believe more in the scissors than I do in the pencil.
> ~ Truman Capote

Editing is the last thing you should do before you turn your paper in. Make sure you leave yourself some time for this step—it can make a big difference in how "polished" your paper feels, and therefore also what kind of grade it gets. Remember, though, that this is not the time to worry about the quality of the ideas—just focus on words and sentences. Note that some of what I'm describing here is closer to proofreading than editing, but there's considerable overlap between the two.

First, a few suggestions:

- Work from a printed copy of your paper—it's easier to see errors.

- Read your paper out loud, slowly.

- Read your paper backwards, one sentence at a time. This is useful because it disrupts your usual flow and forces you to focus on each sentence individually. This is particularly helpful if you have grammatical errors.

- Ask a friend to read it and mark obvious problems. If your friend is a good writer, ask her to make other sentence-level suggestions too. Even better, have your friend read the paper out loud to you. Listen for places where she has trouble reading fluidly, which can indicate problems with rhythm and emphasis.

FIND AND CORRECT OBVIOUS ERRORS

See Chapter 4 for common errors that you should be able to correct in editing. Make sure, too, that you have not misspelled anyone's name; when you refer to Jane Smiley as *Jane Smily*, your professor will doubt your ability to pay close attention to details.

THE DANGERS OF SPELL CHECK Spell Check is useful, of course, but it doesn't replace common sense. For example, if you misspell *definitely* (as many people do), Spell Check will frequently offer *defiantly* as the first option to correct your error. But this is an entirely different word, with a very different meaning. If you blindly accept every suggestion Spell Check makes without thinking about the word, you're likely to end up with some ridiculous mistakes. As always, think for yourself.

CUT USELESS WORDS AND PHRASES

I know, you're trying to get *up* to your professor's minimum length requirement. And now I'm telling you to cut words. But it's worth it—professors appreciate crisply written prose that doesn't include wasted words. (I should, for example, change the end of that sentence to this: *doesn't waste words.*)

Useless words

Inexperienced writers often use a lot of words and phrases that don't add anything to their sentences. They're filler—get rid of them. (The worst offenders are the first five, in bold.)

really	individual	all things considered
very	specific	in a manner of speaking
basically	type of	as a matter of fact
actually	particular	definitely
kind of	in the process of	as it were
sort of	more or less	
generally	for the most part	

More words that can replace phrases

All of the words below in bold are appropriate for academic writing, whereas the words in the two columns to the right are often used when writers are trying to make their sentences sound more impressive (without actually *saying* anything impressive).

because	for the reason that the reason for due to the fact that in light of the fact that	on account of considering the fact that on the grounds that because of the fact that
when	on the occasion of under circumstances in which	in a situation in which
about	as regards with regard to where _____ is concerned	in reference to concerning the matter of
now / today	at this point in time in this day and age	at the present time
must / should	it is crucial that there is a need/necessity for	it is necessary that it is important that
can	is able to has the capacity for	has the opportunity to has the ability to
may / might	it is possible that it could happen that	there is a chance that the possibility exists for

REWRITE FOR CLARITY AND PRECISION

VAGUE LANGUAGE: IT, THIS, THINGS, ETC.

My colleague Elizabeth Trobaugh strictly limits the use of the word *this* in student papers. Her opposition to the word is well-reasoned: Writers frequently fail to be clear what words like *it*, *this*, *things*, and *issues* refer to. Or they have a vague idea but don't take the time to be specific about the reference. Here's an example from a recent student paper:

> So maybe other cultures have **things** we don't. Sometimes they are heavily valued, other times not so much. In **this** case **it** is.

What *things*? In *which* case *what* is? Be specific. As a writer, your job is to make it as easy as possible for the reader to understand what you have to say. (I can't even offer you a revised version of that sentence because I don't know what, exactly, the writer was trying to say.)

Here's an example I can revise, from a student essay about obesity in America:

> David Zinczenko grew up with a "daily choice between McDonalds, Taco Bell, and Kentucky Fried Chicken." He believes that **it** isn't the eater's fault. **It's** the issue that fast food restaurants are everywhere and Americans have no choice, but to eat **it**.

> **Revised:**

> David Zinczenko grew up with a "daily choice between McDonalds, Taco Bell, and Kentucky Fried Chicken." He believes that **teen obesity** isn't the eater's fault. Because fast food restaurants are everywhere, Americans have no choice but to eat **unhealthy foods**.

THERE IS / THERE ARE

These constructions are a poor way to begin a sentence—they tend to be weak because they allow you to avoid saying anything about your subject. For example:

> There is a reason why good writers avoid empty phrases.

What's the reason? Why not tell us in the same sentence?

> Good writers avoid empty phrases because readers resent being forced to read unnecessary words.

"TO BE" VERBS

One of my high school teachers made us write an entire paper without using any "to be" verbs. In other words, we couldn't use *am, is, was, were, are, been, being,* or *be.* It's difficult not to use these verb forms because they're the most common verbs in the English language. (In that sentence, I used two: It *is* difficult, and they *are* the most common....)

I wouldn't suggest that you try to eliminate *all* of these verbs in your writing, but it can be helpful to replace as many of them as possible with stonger, more expressive verbs. Here's an example, using my sentence from above:

> It's difficult not to use these verb forms because . . . .

As I thought about how to get rid of that first *is*, I couldn't just think of a synonym for *is difficult*. I had to think about the entire concept and try to express it differently. Here's what I came up with, and it's no accident that I think the revision is superior:

> We rely on these verb forms because . . . .

Or, if you didn't want to use *We* :

> Writers rely on these verb forms because . . . .

USING DASHES

The dash is a way of separating information. The key difference between the dash and other "separating" marks of punctuation (commas, semi-colons, periods) is that the dash is a stronger interruption, and it generally feels less formal than those other marks. A word on what a dash is *not*: it's not a hyphen. A hyphen is a punctuation mark that connects two or more words: re-create, ex-wife, door-to-door salesman.

Like other marks of punctuation, the dash has grammatical rules that apply to it. These rules depend on whether you use a single dash or a pair, so I'll discuss these separately.

A dash always calls some attention to itself, so you should use it sparingly. It's particularly useful when your sentence includes a number of commas; the dash, or paired dashes, can help keep the grammar of your sentence clear.

SINGLE DASH

> Emily walked away from the restaurant—and away from an entire way of life.

Here, the dash allows you to add another piece of information to the sentence. It could have been done with a comma instead of a dash, but the dash provides more emphasis. It gives the second part of the sentence more weight and importance. A single dash can also allow the part after the dash to function as a definition (not in a dictionary sense) or explanation of what precedes it, like this:

> They made a list of the blockbusters over the decades—the first Tonka trucks, the Frisbee, the Hula-Hoop, the Rubik's Cube.
>
> – Hanna Rosin, "The Touch-Screen Generation," *The Atlantic*, April 2013

In that sentence, what comes after the dash gives examples of the blockbusters; Rosin could also have used a colon (:) instead of the dash. A comma in place of the dash, though, would have made the sentence confusing because of the three commas that separate the toys. The dash is the perfect choice here.

Here's another example from the same article; in this usage, the dash allows the writer to add information and call attention to it.

> The gathering was organized by Warren Buckleitner, a longtime reviewer of interactive children's media who likes to bring together developers, researchers, and interest groups—and often plenty of kids, some still in diapers.
>
> – Hanna Rosin, "The Touch-Screen Generation," *The Atlantic*, April 2013

There's one other way that a single dash can be used, and it's a bit unusual grammatically in that it allows the writer to connect two complete thoughts:

> Also, they were not really meant to teach you something specific—they existed mostly in the service of having fun.
>
> – Hanna Rosin, "The Touch-Screen Generation," *The Atlantic*, April 2013

In that sentence, the part that comes after the dash is a complete thought, which means that in this case the dash has the same grammatical "power" as a period or semicolon.

TIP: WORD PROCESSING

Creating a dash. . . It seems simple, but word processing programs don't always do what you want them to. This usually works:

Type two hyphens immediately after Kevin—don't use the space bar.	Emily walked away from Kevin--
Start typing the next word, again with no spaces after the hyphens. Once you've typed the next word and then hit the space bar, the hyphens will turn into a dash.	Emily walked away from Kevin—and away from everything he represented.

PAIRED DASHES

When you use dashes in a pair, remember that they function almost exactly like parentheses. Grammatically, the principle is identical: Whatever you put inside the dashes can be removed without affecting the grammar of the sentence.

In terms of meaning, too, paired dashes resemble parentheses. What you find inside the dashes is something of an afterthought, an aside, something interesting but not essential to the sentence. What the paired dashes do that parentheses don't is call more attention to the information inside them. Parentheses are like a whispered comment, while dashes are like a poke in the ribs.

> ReD is one of a handful of consultancies that treat everyday life—and everyday consumerism—as a subject worthy of the scrutiny normally reserved for academic social science.
>
> — Graeme Wood, "Anthropology Inc.," *The Atlantic*, March 2013

The information inside the dashes here is an additional piece of information that's not critical to the sentence; however, in placing this brief phrase inside the dashes, the writer has brought more attention to the idea of consumerism.

Here's another example that works in a similar way.

> Still, given the food industry's power to tinker with and market food, we should not dismiss its ability to get unhealthy eaters—slowly, incrementally—to buy better food.
>
> — David H. Freedman, "How Junk Food Can End Obesity," *The Atlantic*, July 2013

And finally, an example of how paired dashes can help you create a lengthy, complex sentence.

> The study adds to a river of evidence suggesting that for the first time in modern history—and in spite of many health-related improvements in our environment, our health care, and our nondietary habits—our health prospects are worsening, mostly because of excess weight.
>
> — David H. Freedman, "How Junk Food Can End Obesity," *The Atlantic*, July 2013

This sentence would be somewhat demanding for many readers, but I do think it holds together well—and it does so in large part because of its sophisticated use of dashes.

TRANSITIONS

BETWEEN PARAGRAPHS

You've probably heard that you're supposed to have transitions between paragraphs, but what does that mean exactly? In short, it means that there's a link between the ideas in one paragraph and the ideas in the next.

The example below, from a student paper, shows the final sentence of a paragraph about low wages for Wal-Mart employees, and then the beginning of next paragraph, which focuses on the lack of health insurance options for those employees.

> ... It is the greed of the management of this company that keeps their workers earning below poverty wages.
>
> Many of the employees at Wal-Mart are unable to get an adequate health plan for themselves and their families due to the high cost of health care. ...

The original has no transition between the two paragraphs, but it's pretty easy to create a link between those ideas. The simplest way to do it is to use an idea from the last sentence of the first paragraph, briefly, in the first sentence of the next paragraph.

> ... It is the greed of the management of this company that keeps their workers earning below poverty wages.
>
> Low wages are only part of the problem, though, because many Wal-Mart employees are unable to get an adequate health plan for themselves and their families due to the high cost of health care. ...

A different version, one that makes a closer connection between the two issues:

> ... It is the greed of the management of this company that keeps their workers earning below poverty wages.
>
> With such low wages, most Wal-Mart employees are also effectively cut off from adequate health care for themselves and their families. ...

BETWEEN SENTENCES

Many writers assume that transitions appear only in the first sentence of a new paragraph, but you need them between (and often within) sentences too.

> Wal-Mart's health insurance covers only 50.2 percent of their 1.4 million U.S. employees. The industry average is 65 percent of workers insured.

The key to making a good transition between these two sentences is to think about how the ideas relate to one another. These ideas are in contrast, so you want a transitional word or phrase that shows that contrast:

> Wal-Mart's health insurance covers only 50.2 percent of their 1.4 million U.S. employees **whereas** the industry average is 65 percent.

TRANSITIONAL WORDS / PHRASES

SIMILARITY	ADDITIONAL SUPPORT	CONTRAST	CAUSE AND EFFECT
likewise			accordingly
similarly			consequently
also	additionally	but	hence
too	again	however	so
just as	also	in contrast	thus
	and	on the other hand	therefore
EMPHASIS	as well	whereas	
certainly	equally important	on the contrary	EXAMPLE
even	further	nevertheless	for example
indeed	furthermore	still	for instance
in fact	in addition	yet	namely
of course	moreover		specifically
truly			to illustrate

DIRECTNESS: AVOIDING STUPID WRITING

The worst kind of bad writing is that which tries to make itself sound smarter or more complex than it actually is, like this:

> Interest in the possible applicability of TRIZ tools and techniques to the world of management and organizational innovation issues continues to grow.

Some of you may be impressed by that—you may think it's sophisticated and complex. It's complicated, that's for sure. But only in the structure of the sentence, not in content. Using that sentence, I'll show you the four key principles for bad writing.

How to write badly in four simple steps

1. **Remove any human presence**: The sentence is "disembodied," which means that it doesn't have a "body," or person. The first word of the sentence is *interest*, so who's interested? Businesses, I assume, so why not say so? Some writers seem to think that if you remove human beings from sentences, the writing will sound smarter. But all it really does is make the sentence harder to understand.

2. **Turn verbs into nouns (also known as nominalization)**: *Applicability* is a nominalization of the verb *apply*; *innovation* is a nominalization of *innovate*.

3. **Use more words than you need**: *Possible* and *the world of* are not needed in this sentence.

4. **Move the verb as far away from the subject as you can**: The subject is *interest*, and the verb is *continues*; there are eighteen words between the two, which makes it extremely difficult to connect them. Our most basic desire in English sentences is for a subject and a verb, preferably close together.

* * *

The guiding principle of the writing in that TRIZ sentence is this: If it's hard to read, you must have to be smart in order to write it. Good writers know that this principle is wrong; furthermore, following it reveals a contempt for the reader. When politicians and business owners communicate with you in this way, you should demand to know why they want to make their policies and practices harder rather than easier to understand. Do they have something to hide?

Here's how the TRIZ sentence could be written more clearly, without any loss of meaning:

> Businesses can become more innovative in management and organization when they apply TRIZ tools and techniques.

I'm not absolutely certain I've said what the original writer intended—but that's because his/her writing is unclear. At any rate, I think I'm close. And I've taken a sentence that was twenty-two words and reduced it to fifteen words (32 percent more efficient!); also, it has a real subject (businesses), followed immediately by a verb, and this combination of changes makes the sentence far easier to read.

English is a flexible, adaptable language, but when writers violate the principles that make it work, they create sentences that don't communicate effectively.

FINAL THOUGHTS

Does this scenario sound familiar? You've waited until the day before a paper is due to start working on it. You stay up until three in the morning to finish it, get a few hours sleep, finish the works-cited page, give it a title, and print it. You rush to campus, make it to class just in time, and triumphantly hand in your paper.

Then, when you get the paper back, you see that the professor has marked several mistakes you could've found if you'd left yourself more time. And the grade reflects all those careless mistakes. (In my class, a sloppy paper with more than a couple of careless errors will rarely get a grade above a C.)

Take time to edit and proofread—at least an hour, if not more. Also, the more time you can allow to pass before doing the editing, the better. If you have a little distance from your work, you're more likely to notice problems.

Turning in a polished paper—even one with some flaws in thinking—is almost sure to get you a better grade than one with obvious errors and awkward sentences.

chapter 6

RESEARCH BASICS

Research means that you don't know, but are willing to find out.
~ Charles Kettering

True genius resides in the capacity for evaluation of uncertain, hazardous, and conflicting information.

~ Winston Churchill

WHY DO YOU HAVE TO WRITE RESEARCH PAPERS?

To get a grade

Of course this is why you write papers, but if you're *only* writing for a grade, you're unlikely to do your best work. Writing formal papers is an important part of college for some good reasons, like these:

It makes you smarter

A confession: When I was a college student majoring in philosophy, I never enjoyed writing papers. I loved seeing the connections among ideas, and how one philosopher's thinking extended or transformed someone else's work, but I often dreaded the writing. I'd done all the important work of learning about a subject, so why did I have to write about it?

I came to understand, slowly, that it was in the writing that I was really learning how to make sense of what I'd read. Don't get me wrong—I love the idea of reading purely for pleasure. But at the heart of higher education is a different way of interacting with ideas. And that kind of interaction *requires* writing.

In short, some of our most significant learning takes place when we write.

It improves the world

In Chapter 2, I said that all writing is rhetorical, meaning that at some level it is always trying to persuade the reader to accept the view(s) of the writer.

When a piece of writing is published as an essay or book, it becomes part of what might be called a "larger conversation," and it's in this conversation that writers have the power to improve the world. For example, when Michael Pollan wrote *The Omnivore's Dilemma*, about how agriculture works in America, he was continuing an ongoing conversation about how farms, industry, business, the environment, the oil industry, and our dining rooms are connected. Plenty of people disagreed with him—but in that disagreement, too, the conversation continued. Pollan doesn't get the last word in the conversation, but he's now part of it, and as a result, people are talking about these issues in new ways. In a not-so-small way, Pollan has changed the world.

Of course, when you write a paper for a college class, that paper isn't likely to be published and influence how people think about a subject. But if you try to think in those terms, it might help you write more purposeful papers.

EXTENDING THE CONVERSATION

Your reader (that mythical stranger who is interested in your subject matter but doesn't know you—and is not your professor) has two basic expectations about your paper:

1. You have something to say.

This means that your paper is driven by an idea that is at least somewhat new or original. It can't simply say what has been said before—why bother writing it if someone else already has?

2. You are aware of what has already been said.

In order for an intelligent reader to trust you, you must demonstrate that you're familiar with the important work that has been already been done on your subject.

If you think of any particular subject—global warming, the effects of technology on higher education, or how Millennials are changing the workplace—you can easily imagine it as a "conversation." One observer says one thing; another person responds to it, perhaps disagrees. Another commentator comes along and enters the conversation by disagreeing with both of the previous thinkers. And so on. The conversation moves in new directions, considers new evidence, continues to evolve. Sometimes the conversation becomes angry and unpleasant, but it's still a conversation. No one ever has the last word.

It's easy to see how this way of thinking about writing and research has implications beyond the classroom. Only in a country that preserves real intellectual freedom can ideas be debated so freely. By extension, when your professor asks you to write a paper, he is asking you to participate in one of the most important forms of democracy available to us: the ability to think freely and share ideas.

INTERACTING WITH SOURCE MATERIAL

When you interact with your sources, you're doing two things—first, announcing to your reader, "Here's what someone else has to say," and second, in effect, saying, "Here's what I have to say about that."

Writing a paper where you only do the first part—reporting what other people have said/written—is generally pointless. (Some professors do assign papers that are merely reports, though, so make sure you know what your professor expects.)

"Here's what someone else has to say."

When you use source material, it's important that you do so responsibly, which means quoting, paraphrasing, or summarizing accurately. Typically, you want to use a *signal phrase* (such as "According to Michael Pollan…") to introduce the source material; this will make it clear that the idea or information belongs to a source, not to you.

Summarize: to state the main idea of a text (or part of a text) in a shortened form.

> **Note:** Usually a summary is only a fraction of the length of the original; you can summarize a three-page essay in a few sentences, but you can't summarize it in three pages—the summary must be a small fraction of the total. For a longer work, like a 300-page novel, you can summarize it in a few sentences or a few paragraphs, depending on how much detail you go into.

Paraphrase: to put someone else's idea into your own words.

Quote: to use the exact words of your source.

"Here's what I have to say about that."

This is where you enter the conversation, and essentially you have three options, with some overlap:

- to use the source in support of something you're saying
- to disagree with an assertion from a source
- to extend or build upon an idea from a source

It should always be clear to your reader *why* you're using source material—it should be in service of an idea you're developing in your paper.

How much source material should your paper have?

The answer to this question depends on a number of factors—the discipline (psychology, linguistics, art history, biology, etc.) you're working in, the type of paper you're writing, your professor's expectations, and so on.

For most research papers, roughly 20 to 50 percent of the paper should come from sources. The other 50 to 80 percent should be you interpreting the evidence and directing our thinking.

Primary vs. secondary sources

Many professors will require that you do both primary (meaning first or original) and secondary research. In the excerpt you're about to read, from Michael Pollan's book, his research on prices of particular items at a grocery store is *primary* research. Most likely, he took notes in a grocery store and/or examined advertising from stores. He didn't rely on some other researcher for this information—he examined the "data" himself. If, however, you use Pollan's book as a source, then his book and everything in it would be a *secondary* source for you.

Primary sources are often pure data (a government census, enrollment figures at a college, city tax records), but they can also be documents created or recorded by "participants" in an event: letters from Civil War soldiers, video of the Kennedy assasination, etc.

Secondary sources, on the other hand, are those that interpret, comment on, analyze, or make arguments about those events: a book that argues how Confederate soldiers became increasingly hopeless as the war progressed, an essay proposing a new theory about Kennedy's death, and so on.

TIP: FINDING & EVALUATING SOURCES

The easier a source is to find, the less reliable and scholarly it tends to be.

Effort and/or Expertise Needed to Find Source		Quality of Source
Minimal effort No expertise	**Quick Google Search / Wikipedia** You can find a Wikipedia entry in a matter of seconds. It will give you some basic (though potentially inaccurate) information, and your professor will think little of it as a source.	Poor
Minimal effort Some expertise	**More Selective Google Search** With slightly more effort, you can find some material on the Internet that's more reliable— articles from a reputable newspaper or magazine (e.g., the *New York Times* or the *The Atlantic*), even some government documents.	Good to Excellent
Some effort Some expertise	**Books** Books typically are not quite as up-to-date as many online resources, but they often explore topics more deeply and thoroughly. Also, if you go to the library, you can consult with research librarians—and take advantage of their expertise at finding resources you likely wouldn't have thought to consult.	Good to Excellent
Some effort Some expertise	**Academic Journals** The most academically respected sources are peer-reviewed academic journals. Search for these in Google Scholar (see Chapter 7) and the library databases (see Chapter 9)—they're not always easy to find or search, but the effort is worth it.	Generally Excellent

SUMMARIZING, PARAPHRASING, AND QUOTING

These three skills are essential in research writing. I'll cover ea
and to illustrate I'll use an excerpt from Michael Pollan's bo
agriculture in America, *The Omnivore's Dilemma*. The following excerpt appears
on page 136, in a chapter that discusses how organic food has become a big
industry. With all three techniques, it's important to provide the proper citation
For more on citations, see Chapter 10: MLA Documentation or Chapter 11:
APA Documentation.

This following excerpt explores how pricing works in traditional supermarkets.

> Wordy labels, point-of-purchase brochures, and certification
> schemes are supposed to make an obscure and complicated
> food chain more legible to the consumer. In the industrial food
> economy, virtually the only information that travels along the food
> chain linking producer and consumer is price. Just look at the
> typical newspaper ad for a supermarket. The sole quality on display
> here is actually a quantity: tomatoes $0.69 a pound; ground chuck
> $1.09 a pound; eggs $0.99 a dozen—special this week. Is there
> any other category of product sold on such a reductive basis? The
> bare-bones information travels in both directions, of course, and
> farmers who get the message that consumers care only about price
> will themselves care only about yield. This is how a cheap food
> economy reinforces itself.

SUMMARIZING

The goal of summarizing is to capture the main idea of the source material—
whether it's a paragraph, a chapter, or an entire book—as accurately as possible.
Remember that your summary must be shorter than what you're summarizing.
In this example, I've reduced seven sentences to one:

signal phrase

Pollan asserts that the industrial food economy continues to dominate because
neither farmers nor traditional grocery stores are motivated to provide any
information beyond price to consumers (136).

You might find it reassuring to know that it took me—the supposed expert in
these matters—about five minutes to write that one sentence. I had to keep
thinking about which information to include and how the ideas related to each
other. I wrote it three different ways before I was satisfied with it.

In a typical research paper, you might use four or five (or many more) sources. Every time you move from one source to another, it's a

THE IMPORTANCE OF SIGNAL PHRASES

moment of potential confusion for the reader, particularly when you're also making your own assertions. When you use signal phrases consistently, it helps the reader keep track of who's saying what.

USEFUL VERBS . . . all are better than *says / states*

asserts   claims   argues   suggests   observes   maintains

PARAPHRASING

To paraphrase is to put a writer's idea in your own words. Most students go about this in the most counter-productive way: they stare at the original sentence and try to think of synonyms for the key words, then put together a "new" sentence that has different words but often sounds awkward.

Instead, the best way to paraphrase is this:

1. Read the sentence(s) closely and be sure that you understand everything the writer is saying. Pay particular attention to how ideas relate to each other, especially when the writer is showing causality (one thing causing another).

2. Close the book, or the web page, or whatever it is you're reading. Reconstruct the idea in your head in language that makes sense to you. If you're not looking at the original, you'll be less inclined to repeat its wording or structure, and the sentence you write will sound more natural.

3. Start writing, still without looking at the original. Don't worry if you repeat a word or two that appeared in the original.

4. Compare your version to the original. The idea from the original should be intact, but the new sentence should sound like *your* writing. Now, if necessary, think of synonyms to replace key words you repeat from the original.

Here's an example where I paraphrase one of Pollan's sentences. His sentence:

> The bare-bones information travels in both directions, of course, and farmers who get the message that consumers care only about price will themselves care only about yield.

First, I made sure I understood the idea—that farmers have changed their practices *because* (causality) they know what motivates consumers.

This is what I came up with. It might not be the finest paraphrase you'll ever read, but it does the job. The ideas are intact, as is the relationship between them, i.e., the cause and effect. And I believe that the voice is mine, not Pollan's.

signal phrase

Pollan asserts that because many farmers believe consumers are only concerned with cost, the farmers then focus only on how much of any particular crop they can produce (136).

Here's another version, without a signal phrase:

Farmers who know that consumers are concerned with cost alone will in turn focus only on how much of any particular crop they can produce (Pollan 136).

SLOPPY PARAPHRASE = PLAGIARISM

If you paraphrase badly, you may be at risk of plagiarizing.

First, be sure that you cite your source properly. Yes, even if you put source material into your own words, you still must give credit to your sources for their ideas. If you don't, it's plagiarism.

Second, be aware that if you follow the sentence structure or language of the original too closely, this may be considered *inappropriate borrowing* and thus also a form of plagiarism. For example, the following paraphrase of the Pollan sentence would be deemed unacceptable by most professors:

Pollan asserts that the basic information moves both ways, so farmers who learn that grocery store customers only care about how much things cost will themselves care only about how much they can produce (136).

Why is this unacceptable? Because it follows the wording of the original too closely. Even though it's properly documented, the language and sentence structure are too similar to Pollan's.

HOW DO YOU DECIDE WHETHER TO QUOTE OR PARAPHRASE?

Your first instinct should be to paraphrase. It's generally better to use your own language—and it's good intellectual practice to put someone else's ideas into your own words.

I'm not saying that you shouldn't quote your sources; quotations are essential, and they can help you be more efficient and accurate. The danger is that when you quote too much, your paper may sound more like a jumble of other writers than *you*.

Here are three good reasons to quote rather than paraphrase:

1. Your source says something in a particularly compelling or interesting way. If the specific language the source uses is important to our understanding of the idea, you should quote that language.

2. Your source says something that is similar to, or supportive of, a point you're making. In this case, the exact words of the source can help back up a claim you're making.

3. Your source says something that you disagree with, and part of your analysis focuses on shades of meaning that can be seen in the precise word choice.

QUOTING

Once you've decided to quote rather than paraphrase, you have one more decision to make: Do you want to quote an entire sentence (or more), or do you want to quote only part of a sentence?

Quoting an entire sentence

This is the easiest way to quote because there are no complicated rules about punctuation. I'll choose a sentence that fits my first reason for quoting—the one that says to quote a writer when he or she says something in a particularly interesting way:

signal phrase

As Michael Pollan observes, "The bare-bones information travels in both directions, of course, and farmers who get the message that consumers care only about price will themselves care only about yield" (136).

It looks simple, but many students make mistakes with this kind o
It's essential that you have some kind of introduction for the quo
should never have a sentence that's only a quotation without any kind of context.
The "context" I've provided, *As Michael Pollan observes*, is minimal; sometimes
you'll want to do more, but generally this is adequate.

Quoting part of a sentence

This is often more effective than quoting an entire sentence. It allows you to
partially paraphrase a writer's idea but still show his or her exact wording, briefly.
Quoting part of a sentence is useful when a writer says something memorable or
interesting—or simply difficult to paraphrase—in just a word or phrase. Here I
quote part of Pollan's first sentence:

signal phrase

Pollan claims that stores like Whole Foods use these techniques to "make an
obscure and complicated food chain more legible to the consumer" (136).

The key to making the partial quotation work is to make the quoted material
flows grammatically within the entire sentence. In other words, if you took the
quotation marks away, the sentence would still make sense grammatically—it
would still sound like a good sentence. (Though, of course, you wouldn't want to
actually do this because that would be plagiarism.)

You can also quote a single word, which puts great emphasis on that word:

Pollan describes the contemporary agricultural economy as "industrial" (136).

When I was writing that sentence, I had the feeling that I wanted to disagree
with Pollan—something about calling attention to that single word *industrial*
made me think that the next sentence should question that word choice.

Of course, I could also have emphasized that word because I wanted to assert
that Pollan's description is accurate and even revealing:

signal phrase

Pollan describes the contemporary agricultural process as "industrial" (136); this
makes plain the connections between farming and big business and reveals their
shared qualities: both are dirty and dangerous.

Reminder: This is just a quick overview of the key things you need to know
about quoting. In Chapters 10 and 11, I cover additional guidelines that you're

likely to need: how to use ellipses (the three dots) and brackets (for words that you change in a quotation), and how to quote someone who's being quoted.

PLAGIARISM

What it is

Plagiarism can take many forms, and some are worse than others. Most simply, it means taking something that is not yours (an idea, a statistic, a piece of research, or an entire paper) and presenting it as your own. This is intellectual theft, and it violates everything that colleges and universities value.

How to avoid it

To begin with, try to find a topic for your research that you care about; I realize that this is sometimes difficult, since many professors choose and/or limit your topics. If you can't choose your own topic, try to find some aspect of the topic that is meaningful to you. When you care about your subject, you're more likely to want to do your own thinking about it.

Plagiarism and research

As you do your research, try to be organized with your sources. Highlight passages that you plan on quoting, paraphrasing, or summarizing. Develop a number or symbol system to help you keep track of sources. I've seen far too many students suffer because they put off doing their in-text citations until they finished writing their papers; this is a terrible idea because at that stage you then have to look up all the sources (and sometimes even the page numbers) again. Maintain a system as you take notes and as you write. When in doubt, give credit to a source; if you're not sure whether or not you need an in-text citation, provide one.

Don't put the paper off until the last minute. A research paper requires careful attention to detail, and it's generally not the kind of thing you can pull off the night before it's due. It's in your best interest to have all of your citations (in-text and a works-cited page) done in your first draft. That way your professor can let you know if there are problems.

chapter 7

INTERNET RESEARCH

Getting information off the Internet is like taking a drink from a fire hydrant.

~ Mitch Kapor

Everyone knows how to search the Internet, but this chapter is meant to help you search more productively and efficiently.

Let's say that you're writing a paper that responds to some issue in Michael Pollan's book *The Omnivore's Dilemma* (see previous chapter for excerpt). For the sake of this example, let's pretend that you've narrowed your topic somewhat and decided to address what Pollan calls the "industrial food economy." Of course, the specific focus of your paper will determine how you search, but let's start with some basic principles.

A BASIC GOOGLE SEARCH

The most obvious thing to do is to search for *industrial food economy*, right? Sure, why not…

TIP Put your search terms inside quotation marks—but only if the words, together, make a phrase that you're likely to find a number of writers using. For example, it would *not* make sense to do this search:

NO Google `"Pollan industrial food economy"` Search

But it *would* make sense to search for this:

YES Google `Pollan "industrial food economy"` Search

In this case, though, because we want to find things that don't necessarily make reference to Pollan, we'll leave out his name. In the search below, we'll only get results that include the exact phrase *industrial food economy*.

EVALUATING THE RESULTS

This is where things become more complicated. I'll offer some strategies for evaluating your search results, but my basic advice is to use both common sense and critical thinking.

Google   "industrial food economy"

All   Images   Videos   News   Shopping   Maps   Books

About 13,500 results

1 Creative Food Economy Emerges in Ontario : TreeHugger
www.treehugger.com/.../creative-food-economy-emerges-in-ontario.html ▾
Mar 9, 2009 ... Features, Old 'Industrial Food' Economy, New 'Creative Food' Economy. Prototypical company, Kraft — cheese products, Craft/artisanal cheese.

2 Organic Economics In A World of Industrial Agriculture: Applying the ...
www.greenmoneyjournal.com/.../organic-economics-in-a-world-of-industrial - agriculture-applying-the-power-of-nature/ ▾
World War II changed everything, laying the foundation for today's **industrial food economy**. With the need to feed millions of soldiers, packaged food production ...

3 Bringing the Food Economy Home « OrganicFoodee.com
www.organicfoodee.com/books/foodeconomy/ ▾
Bringing the Food Economy Home provides an eye-opening analysis of the problems caused by the globalised **industrial food economy**. As the writers point out, ...

4 Reclaiming Food Sovereignty from the Global Economy
faculty.missouri.edu/ikerdj/papers/Hartwick-Food.htm ▾
We have created an industrial economy, including an **industrial food economy**, which is inevitably trending toward entropy. It is simply not sustainable.

5 Wendell Berry: The Pleasures of Eating | ecoliteracy.org
www.ecoliteracy.org/article/wendell-berry-pleasures-eating ▾
Jun 29, 2009 ... For decades now the entire **industrial food economy**, from the large farms and feedlots to the chains of supermarkets and fast-food restaurants ...

6 Organic Economics In A World of Industrial Agriculture: Applying the ...
www.greenmoneyjournal.com/.../organic-economics-in-a-world-of-industrial - agriculture-applying-the-power-of-nature/ ▾
World War II changed everything, laying the foundation for today's **industrial food economy**. With the need to feed millions of soldiers, packaged food production ...

7 Food Politics | Eat Drink Politics
www.eatdrinkpolitics.com/about/resources/food-politics/ ▾
Our **industrial food economy**, led by an increasingly small group of transnational food conglomerates and buffeted by corporate-influenced government policies, ...

Let's look at the first result, from TreeHugger.com.

Hamilton Farmers Market. Credit: Communications Branch of the Ontario Ministry of Agriculture and Food

In North America the food economy has long been dominated by commodities. A big part of the sustainable and local food movement is a direct response to systems that are controlled by outside interests. New models for food system are continually

The title, "Creative Food Economy Emerges in Ontario," makes me think that this probably isn't a great source for my paper, mainly because the focus on Ontario (part of Canada) makes the subject matter too narrow. Also, at the bottom of the page, I can see who publishes the site:

© TreeHugger.com 2010 | Visitor Agreement | Privacy Policy | Discovery Communications, LLC

Discovery Sites: Discovery Channel | TLC | Animal Planet | Discovery Health | Science Channel | Discovery Store Planet Green | HowStuffWorks | Discovery Times | Discovery Kids | HD Theater | FitTV | Petfinder | Turbo

The "publisher" is TreeHugger.com, which means nothing to me. But I also see that the site is connected to the Discovery Channel, which means that it's more about entertainment (and profit) than education or serious research. Hey, I'm not picking on Discovery Channel—I watch it myself and find it interesting and informative. But I wouldn't rely on it as a source for a research paper.

Two sites, compared

Here are the third and fourth results from the search:

> **Bringing the Food Economy Home « OrganicFoodee.com**
> www.organicfoodee.com/books/foodeconomy/ ▾
> Bringing the Food Economy Home provides an eye-opening analysis of the problems caused by the globalised **industrial food economy**. As the writers point out, ...

> **Reclaiming Food Sovereignty from the Global Economy**
> faculty.missouri.edu/ikerdj/papers/Hartwick-Food.htm ▾
> We have created an industrial economy, including an **industrial food economy**, which is inevitably trending toward entropy. It is simply not sustainable.

"Bringing the Food Economy Home" sounds like a reasonably serious title for a page, but the name of the site, OrganicFoodee.com, does not inspire confidence. It sounds informal and casual, not academic or scholarly. The fourth result, on the other hand, "Reclaiming Food Sovereignty from the Global Economy," sounds more academic. Also notice that the URL is faculty.missouri.edu, the website of a large research university. Not every site that ends in .edu will offer reliable information, though, so you should investigate further before you assume that the source will be appropriate.

Let's look at both pages more closely to determine if either of them would be useful as a source for a college paper.

TIP Use the hyphen key (which also functions as the minus key) to eliminate terms you don't want Google to search for. Because I was getting too many results related to grocery stores, I later used this technique to tell Google not to search for *grocery*, which gave me better results:

 industrial food economy -grocery   🔍

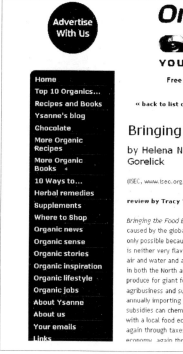

YOUR ORGANIC LIFESTYLE MAGAZINE

Free Organic Newsletter! Sign up here »   Search

« back to list of articles

Bringing the Food Economy Home

by Helena Norberg-Hodge, Todd Merrifield and Steven Gorelick

(ISEC, www.isec.org.uk)

review by Tracy Worcester

Bringing the Food Economy Home provides an eye-opening analysis of the problems caused by the globalised industrial food economy. As the writers point out, this system is only possible because of a whole range of hidden subsidies, and 'it is giving us food that is neither very flavourful nor nutritious, at a price that includes depleted soil, poisoned air and water and a destabilised global climate'. In addition, livelihoods and communities in both the North and South are being destroyed as farmers are pitted against farmers to produce for giant food corporations. Our food economy, in the stranglehold of agribusiness and supermarkets, is 'absurdly inefficient' with many examples of Britain annually importing roughly the same amount of food as it exports. Only through massive subsidies can chemical and energy intensive food carted round the globe be competitive with a local food economy. The consumer pays four times: once at the supermarket till, again through taxes to help farmers compete with the artificially low prices in the global economy, again through taxes to build energy and transport infrastructure and again for

The fact that the site calls itself "your organic lifestyle magazine" should confirm what I suggested earlier—namely, that it wouldn't be a very reliable source of information. This is not to say that you couldn't learn from the site, or even get ideas for your paper. But it's not the kind of source you want for most college papers. However, if you're writing about the popularity of organic food, then you might find it useful to examine the popularity and profitability of sites like this.

You should also notice that what appears on this page is actually a review of a book, and maybe the book would be worth reading for your research. In short, even pages that don't look useful can contain something worth exploring. But do so cautiously, and always with an awareness of the quality of sources you intend to use in your paper. Your reader wouldn't take your paper seriously if all of your sources were like OrganicFoodee.com.

Now let's look at the fourth result more closely.

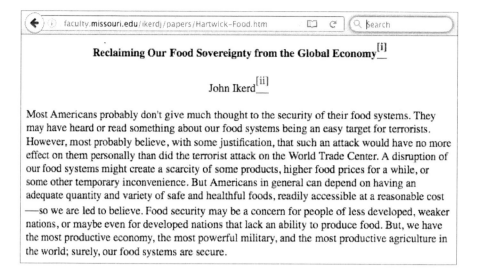

This is just the first paragraph of a long document. Is it a source you could use? How do you decide? There are two key questions that will help you determine how reliable it is as a potential source: Who publishes the site, and who wrote the material you're reading?

Who publishes the site?

We already know that this site is from the University of Missouri. If you go to the bottom of the page, there's no publisher listed—but there is other information that may be helpful.

[i] Presented at Hartwick College guest lecture series, Food in Our Lives, Oneonta, NY, November 3, 2005.

[ii] John Ikerd is Professor Emeritus, University of Missouri, Columbia, MO USA; author of, *Sustainable Capitalism: A Matter of Common Sense*, http://kpbooks.com; website: http://www.ssu.missouri.edu/faculty/jikerd.

[iii] For a complete discussion of differences in industrial and sustainable systems, see John Ikerd, *Sustainable Capitalism: A Matter of Common Sense*, 2005, Kumarian Press, Inc., Bloomfield, CT, available through <http://kpbooks.com>.

The first note tells me that the paper was presented as a lecture at a college, which makes it seem relatively trustworthy.

Who wrote what you're reading?

If you look at the second note, above, you see that the author is a professor and that he has written a book on a related topic. These are both good signs. Again, it doesn't mean that what this lecture says is *true*, but it does mean that it's a reasonable source to use in a college paper.

If you're not sure what kind of qualifications the author has, do a Google search and see if you can find out who he works for and where he's been published. If the sources are all blogs, for example, you should probably rule him out as a serious source. If, however, he's had his work published in reputable newspapers and magazines, he could be a good general commentator on your topic. If he's a working scholar who publishes articles in academic journals, then he's definitely a good source.

Wikipedia?

Intensive animal farming or industrial **livestock** production, also called **factory farming** by opponents of the practice, is a modern form of **intensive farming** that refers to the keeping of **livestock**, such as **cattle**, poultry (including in "battery cages") and fish at higher stocking densities than is usually the case with ...

Intensive animal farming - Wikipedia, the free encyclopedia
https://en.wikipedia.org/wiki/**Intensive_animal_farming** Wikipedia

About this result · Feedback

Intensive animal farming - Wikipedia, the free encyclopedia
https://en.wikipedia.org/wiki/**Intensive_animal_farming** Wikipedia
Intensive animal farming or industrial **livestock** production, also called **factory farming** by opponents of the practice, is a modern form of **intensive farming** that refers to the keeping of **livestock**, such as cattle, poultry (including in "battery cages") and fish at higher stocking densities than is usually the case with ...

No matter what you search for, it seems, Wikipedia is likely to have an entry. In general, you should use Wikipedia only for background information, and you should verify anything you read there with other sources. (You did know that *anyone* can write or edit almost all Wikipedia entries, right? The obvious result of this very democratic approach is that errors—some created by people to amuse themselves, others because they have some kind of agenda—are common.) Most professors do not want to see Wikipedia as a source in your papers.

INTERNET SEARCHES BY AUTHOR AND TITLE

If you've narrowed your paper topic somewhat, you should have some good search terms already. If you don't, though, here are two suggestions for other ways to search:

Author name: Do a search for the author of anything you've read on your topic. Often, the author has written other works that may explore similar or related subject matter. You'll also find other writers commenting on that author's work.

Work title: This is the same principle as searching for an author's name. If it's a book, you're certain to find book reviews (below), which can be useful.

Searching for the title, *The Omnivore's Dilemma*, brought me to a commentary essay in which the writer objects to Pollan's ideas; it would make a good (though not scholarly) source for a paper on this subject.

> An economist's critique of **The Omnivore's Dilemma** - By Tyler ...
> Nov 1, 2006 ... In **The Omnivore's Dilemma**: A Natural History of Four Meals, food writer and UC-Berkeley professor Michael Pollan examines three American ...
> www.**slate**.com/id/2152675/ - Cached - Similar

SEARCHING BEYOND GOOGLE

Okay, not exactly *beyond* Google, but beyond the ways most of us ordinarily use Google. This section will introduce you to Google Scholar and Google Books, two great resources that are easy to use.

GOOGLE SCHOLAR

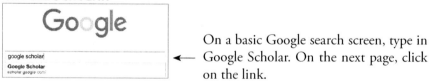

On a basic Google search screen, type in Google Scholar. On the next page, click on the link.

The results that you see on the next page are quite different from the previous searches, mainly in that they're all scholarly articles. These aren't necessarily the only kinds of sources you need in college papers, but they are ones you should learn how to find and use routinely. Quoting from an article in *Time* magazine is fine up to a point, but when you quote from scholarly sources, your reader will take you more seriously.

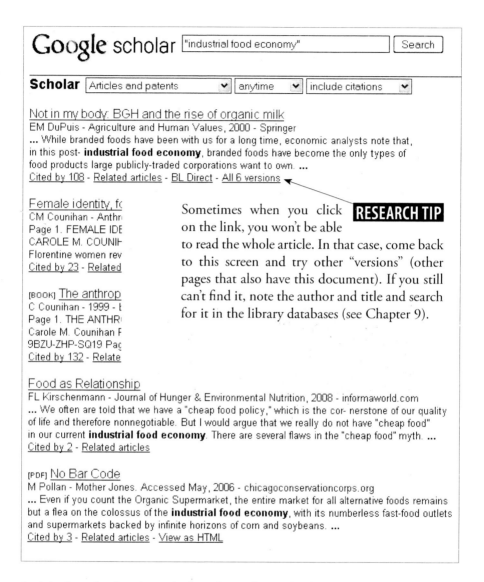

Let's look at the fourth result, "Food as Relationship."

Name of journal that
published the article

Article title → **Food** as Relationship

Author

FL Kirschenmann - Journal of Hunger & Environmental Nutrition, 2008 - informaworld.com
... **Food** always becomes part of the ecology from which it is produced. Page 4. Frederick L.
Kirschenmann 109 **FOOD** IN THE **INDUSTRIAL ECONOMY** The soil/**food**/health connection
is not the only relationship we ignore in our modern **food** system. ...
Cited by 2 - Related articles

Unlike a regular web page, a typical result from a Google Scholar search will take you straight to the article, but sometimes you'll only get an abstract (see below for definition), as is the case here.

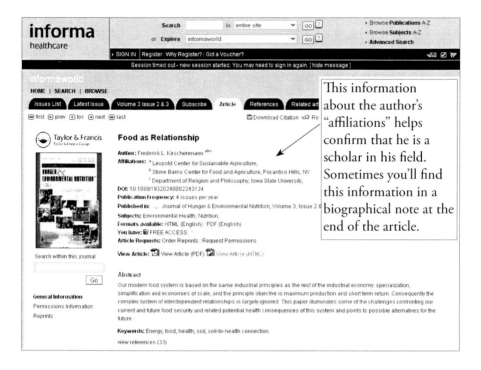

This information about the author's "affiliations" helps confirm that he is a scholar in his field. Sometimes you'll find this information in a biographical note at the end of the article.

WHAT'S A PDF?

PDF stands for "portable document format," and it means that you're seeing a picture of the original document. One advantage of a PDF is that it's easier to cite as a source. See Chapter 10.

WHAT'S AN ABSTRACT?

An abstract is a brief summary of an academic article. It's useful because it tells you, quickly, what the article is about as well as the basic argument the author is trying to make. In the sciences, abstracts also tell you how the author conducted the research.

Reading the abstract will give you a sense of the writer's style as well. In some cases, you might rule out an article if you can tell from the abstract that it's too advanced. If you do want to read the rest of the article, you have a couple of options.

In this case, the site will allow you to look at a PDF of the article, or an HTML (web) page. Given the choice, always opt for the PDF, primarily because it allows you to document the source more accurately (see Chapter 10).

Here's what the PDF looks like. You can enlarge each page for easier reading or print it. Also note the find box; see instructions on next page for using it.

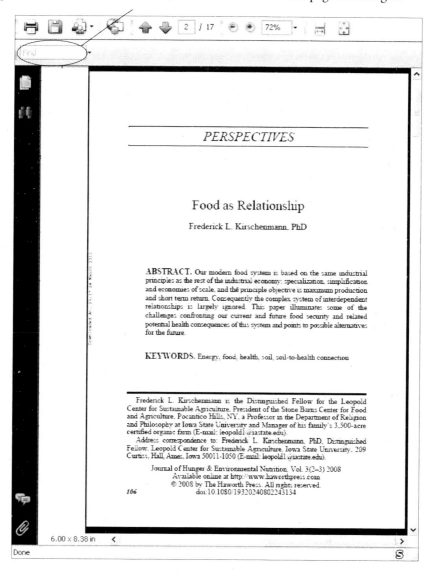

If you're in a hurry (or just a little lazy) . . .

Let's say you want to find where the author of that article talks about industrialization of food. (This is particularly useful when you find articles that only slightly apply to your area of research.)

Use the **Find** function. On normal web pages—or any other document—use CTRL + F. In a PDF document, **Find** is at the top of the screen:

In this case, I put in the word *industrial*. Below you can see one of the places where that word appears. If I hit the ENTER button on the keyboard, it takes me to the next appearance of the word, highlighted in blue.

Frederick L. Kirschenmann   *109*

FOOD IN THE INDUSTRIAL ECONOMY

The soil/food/health connection is not the only relationship we ignore in our modern food system. In fact, our modern industrial culture tends to view not only food but almost all of reality as a collection of fragments (things) rather than a web of relationships. Modern philosophers trace this tendency to the 17th-century scientific revolution. Rene Descartes wanted science to become a "universal mathematics," which, of course, tended to reduce all of reality to measurable things and ignored dynamic relationships. It should not be surprising, therefore, that we have reduced our understanding of healthy food to an ingredient list.

GOOGLE BOOKS

You won't find the full text of every book here, but you can read large excerpts from quite a few, which makes it a great way to preview books before you decide what you want to get at the library. To use it, do a Google search for Google Books, and then click on the first link.

Google Books

https://**books.google**.com/ ▾

Account Options. Sign in. **Books**. Search the world's most comprehensive index of full-text **books**. My library · Publishers About Privacy Terms Help.

Here are some of the results, using the same search terms as before.

Go gle books industrial food economy

The omnivore's dilemma: a natural history of four meals - Page 260

Michael Pollan - Social Science - 2006 - 450 pages
Even if you count the organic supermarket, the entire market for all alternative
foods remains but a flea on the colossus of the **industrial food economy**, ...
Limited preview - About this book - Add to my library - More editions

The End of **Food** - Page 31

Paul Roberts - Business & Economics - 2009 - 432 pages
In a **food economy** geared toward ever lower prices, selling convenience has
become the **food** industry's most important means of making money. ...
Limited preview - About this book - Add to my library - More editions

Food economy in Hungary

Ernő Csizmadia, Magda Székely - Nature - 1986 - 217 pages
Page 52
No preview available - About this book - Add to my library

Deep **economy**: the wealth of communities and the durable future - Page 47

Bill McKibben - Social Science - 2007 - 261 pages
Even today, in a world **economy** that churns out jet airplanes and iPods and laser
... that in the absence of the **industrial food** system I wouldn't starve. ...
Limited preview - About this book - Add to my library - More editions

Bringing the **food economy** home: local alternatives to global agribusiness

Helena Norberg-Hodge, Todd Merrifield, Steven Gorelick - Business & Economics - 2002 - 150 pages
Limited preview - About this book - Add to my library - More editions

Not surprisingly, Michael Pollan's book appears first, as he uses the phrase "industrial food economy" a number of times. (I chose not to include the quotation marks in this search because I got better results—I tried it both ways.)

I found the last book potentially interesting, and it immediately struck me as familiar. Then I remembered that this was the book being reviewed at OnlineFoodee.com. Based on the title and subtitle (*Local Alternatives to Global Agribusiness*), I think it could be an excellent source. I might check to see who the authors are, and make sure that it's published by a legitimate company. Being "published" doesn't necessarily make a book reliable, and some publishers are better than others.

I won't be able to read all of this book on Google Books, but I can certainly see enough of it, including the table of contents, to know if I want to try to find it at a local library.

Bringing the food economy home: local alternatives to global agribusiness By Helen

Overview
› Preview
Reviews (5)
Buy

Contents ▾   Front Cover

Result **1** of **14** in this book for **industrial food economy** - ‹ Previous Next › - Vi

I first click on **Contents** at the top of the page. Here I can see all of the chapter titles.

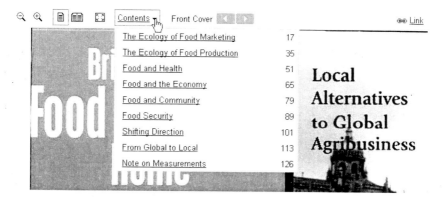

However, when I try to read a few pages into one chapter, I find missing pages:

Pages 53-77 are not part of this book preview

This is pretty common with books on Google. Still, there's a lot of this book that I *can* read, certainly enough to decide if I want to try to find it at the library (see Chapter 8: Library Research).

One more tip

Works-cited entries are a great resource for researchers. Many books—not just scholarly ones—will include a list of sources the author used. Michael Pollan's book has an extensive list of sources; these are some he used in Chapter 2:

> In writing about the rise of industrial agriculture I also drew on the following works:
>
> Kimbrell, Andrew. *The Fatal Harvest Reader: The Tragedy of Industrial Agriculture* (Washington, D.C.: Island Press, 2002).
>
> Manning, Richard. *Against the Grain* (New York: North Point Press, 2004).
>
> Morgan, Dan. *Merchants of Grain* (New York: Viking, 1979).
>
> Russell, Edmund. *War and Nature: Fighting Humans and Insects with Chemicals from World War I to Silent Spring* (Cambridge, U.K.: Cambridge University Press, 2001).
>
> Schwab, Jim. *Raising Less Corn and More Hell: Midwestern Farmers Speak Out* (Urbana: University of Illinois Press, 1988). See the interview with George Naylor beginning on page 111.

A "HYBRID" SEARCH

The great strength of the Internet is in linking—the easy movement from one page to the next, where one idea or subject offers an immediate connection to related ideas. To take advantage of this as a researcher, you might want to try what I call a "hybrid" approach, one that combines an online bookstore, Google Books, and your library. I use Amazon.com because it's the largest, but other companies will work too. Start by finding any book related to your topic at the online bookstore. I chose one from the Google Books search.

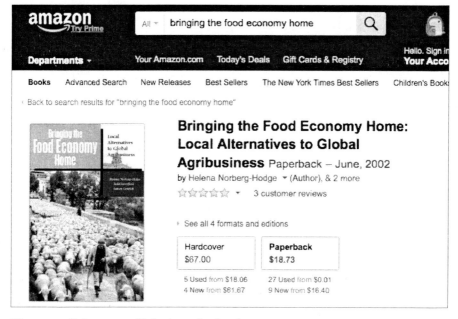

If you scroll down, you'll find similar books:

The second book, *Hungry City*, looks promising. After clicking on it, I was led to even more books that would seem useful for this research.

I continued moving from one book to the next and eventually ended up on this one. The ***Look Inside*** feature allows you to see the table of contents. But first, you should try to determine whether or not this is a quality source.

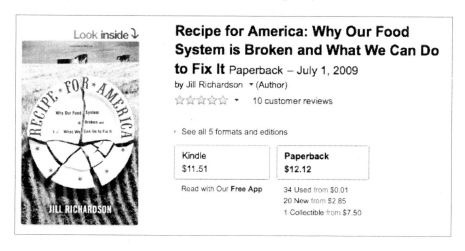

It gets great reviews from Amazon readers, but you can also see what a professional thinks of it by scrolling down to *Editorial Reviews*. A few pages back, I said that reviews weren't always a great source for your paper; I stand by that. In this case, though, I'm suggesting that you use the professional (rather than reader) reviews to help you decide if the book is appropriate for a college research paper.

This review comes from *Publisher's Weekly*, a respected magazine in the publishing world. It contains some revealing insights into the book. First, the book would appear to be more personal, and not very scholarly, which limits its usefulness somewhat. Second, this reviewer is not impressed by the author's skill in constructing an argument. So it might not be a great source for information or careful analysis. But if you're interested in writing about how the "local food" movement has flaws that largely go unquestioned, this book might be useful.

Editorial Reviews

From Publishers Weekly

The evils of industrial agriculture are rehashed in this impassioned but sketchy exposé. Food activist and blogger Richardson ticks off a familiar menu of food-system dysfunctions: overreliance on pesticides and fertilizer, exploited farmers and workers, horribly abused livestock, obese children who are fed subsidized junk food in school. . . . Only the choir will be convinced by Richardson's shallow take on these complex issues.

FINAL THOUGHT

The Internet is a powerful tool for research—so powerful, in fact, that you may wonder why we even need libraries anymore. . . . (But we do; keep reading.)

chapter 8

LIBRARY RESEARCH

I find that a great part of the information I have was acquired by looking something up and finding something else on the way.
~ Franklin P. Adams

Who needs libraries when we have the Internet?

Not long ago, if you wanted to do serious research, you went to the library. You searched through card catalogs for books or the *Reader's Guide to Periodical Literature* for articles. Now, of course, you can do similar research from your home computer or even your phone. But the offerings in Google Books remain limited, particularly with newer releases.

Card catalogs at Sterling Memorial Library, Yale University

As such, you should learn a few ways to make effective use of your library. If you go in person, you can check out an actual book, which—compared to viewing the same material online—some research says is more effective for processing and retaining information.

An even better reason to go the libary isn't for *what* you'll find there, but *who*—namely, reference librarians. They love helping people find information, and they tend to be very, very good at it. Take advantage of their knowledge and resourcefulness.

You still don't necessarily need to physically go to the library because many college libraries also offer live online chatting with reference librarians. Here are some of the options available at HCC:

Ask the Librarian

- **In person or by phone**. For personalized assistance with research or class assignments, visit or phone the Reference Desk. The phone number is (413) 552-2424. Find out when the library is open on our hours page.

- **Text us a question at 413-282-8552**
  We respond to text messages at least once a day when the library is open (the hours page lists our schedule). Although you can ask any question, the service works best for simple, quick questions. If you have a more in depth question or need a more immediate response, please call us at 413-552-2424 or just stop by.

- **Send your question now** to HCC's online reference service **Ask the Librarian** (we'll reply within a business day).

- **Request a consultation with a librarian** HCC students can request a 30-45 minute individual research consultation. Schedule an appointment!

The main library phone number is (413) 552-2372. To contact specific library staff members, consult the Library Staff Directory.

Finally, more and more books are available electronically through your library than ever before. Generally, you can read these books on most computers, tablets, and phones. In some cases, when you might not be able to get a physical copy of a book right away, you can check out the e-book and start reading it within minutes. Aside from convenience, e-books have other benefits. I'll go over some of those later in this chapter.

SEARCHING FOR A BOOK AT YOUR COLLEGE LIBRARY

Building on the previous chapter, let's start with a simple search for a specific author. Go to your college's home page and click on **Library**.

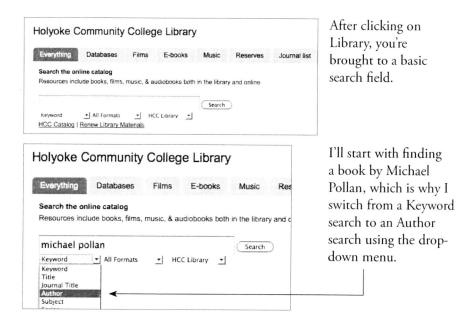

After clicking on Library, you're brought to a basic search field.

I'll start with finding a book by Michael Pollan, which is why I switch from a Keyword search to an Author search using the drop-down menu.

Here are the first three of ten books. Ignore the first one (it's for "young readers").

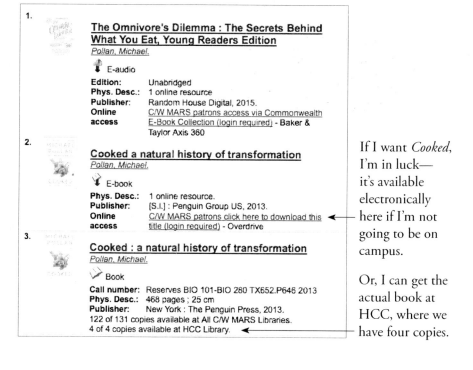

If I want *Cooked*, I'm in luck— it's available electronically here if I'm not going to be on campus.

Or, I can get the actual book at HCC, where we have four copies.

If the library you're searching has the book, make note of the call number.

Location	Call Number / Copy Notes	Text to Phone	Barcode	Shelving Location	Status	Due Date
HCC Library	GT2850.P65 2006	(Text)	38130000126343	General	Available	-

At HCC, most books are on the fourth floor (two floors up from the entrance).

But let's say it's a different book by Pollan that I want:

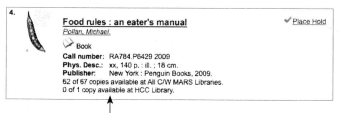

We don't have a copy of this one. But I see in the line above this that the libraries in our regional system have 67 copies, 62 of which are available. Next, I'll click on the title of the book and find out which libraries have the book.

One option is to use the drop-down menu to search a specific library—maybe your local library has a copy.

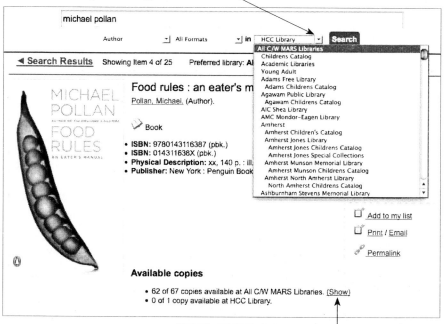

A second option is to click (Show) to see a list of all the libraries that have the book; the list will tell you whether the book is available or checked out.

The final option is to place a "hold" on (in other words, *request*) the book.

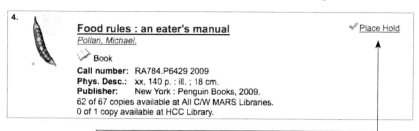

After you click here, you'll enter your library card information and the book will be sent to the HCC library, where you can pick it up in a few days—as long as it's available. If it's a popular book or movie, you may be put on a waiting list, in which case it could take weeks or even months before you get the book.

One last piece of advice: After you've found a book you're interested in, scroll down to see other books that have been identified as similar. Here's what came up under the Pollan book:

A note about books on reserve

On page 113, I said that the HCC library had four copies of this book:

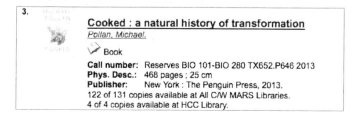

When I opened the next page, though, I found that three of those books were "on reserve."

Location	Call Number / Copy Notes	Text to Phone	Barcode	Shelving Location	Status	Due Date
HCC Library	TX652.P646 2013	(Text)	38130000190653	General	Available	-
HCC Library	Reserves BIO 101-BIO 280 TX652.P646 2013	(Text)	38130000245473	Reserves	Available	-
HCC Library	Reserves BIO 101-BIO 280 TX652.P646 2013	(Text)	38130000245481	Reserves	Available	-
HCC Library	Reserves BIO 101-BIO 280 TX652.P646 2013	(Text)	38130000245499	Reserves	Available	-

In other words, they've been set aside for students in specific biology courses to use. (The one copy that is available will almost certainly be checked out by a biology student during the first week of classes.)

E-BOOKS

As I said at the beginning of this chapter, e-books have some real advantages over physical books. The most obvious is convenience—all you need is a device and an Internet connection (plus the free software or app) to read tens of thousands of books. Another advantage, though, is that you can search an e-book for specific terms relevant to your research. This is often more effective than using the index in a traditional book. Finally, you can highlight passages, make notes, and instantly see definitions of every word in the book.

I'll go over Axis 360 and Overdrive in the next few pages, but you should first know about one of HCC's most powerful book resources. To get there, start by choosing the **E-books** tab.

Choose **searched individually**, which will take you to these sites (and others):

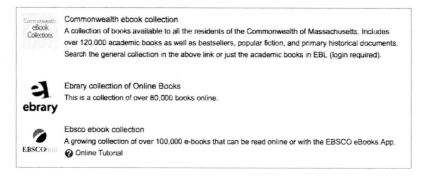

AXIS 360

Here's what it looks like when a book is offered electronically via Axis 360:

Click here.

The page will prompt you to download the software (unless you're using a Mac—though the publisher will probably have software for Mac soon). Here's what you'll see:

Using a phone? You'll want to download these two (small) apps, Axis 360 and Overdrive.

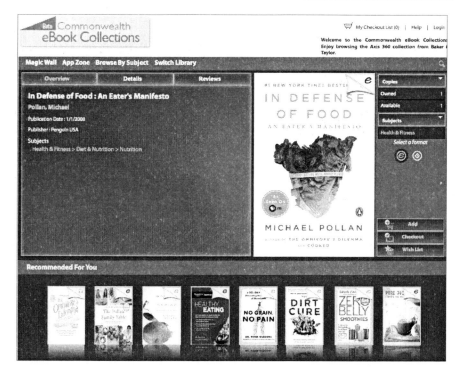

Axis 360 on a phone

After downloading the Axis 360 software to my phone, here's what it looks like:

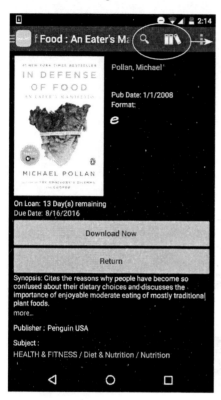

Clicking on the magnifying glass allows you to search the book for words or phrases.

Clicking on the books (or whatever those are supposed to be) to the right shows you what you've checked out.

Note: If you're finished using a book, please return it so it's available for others.

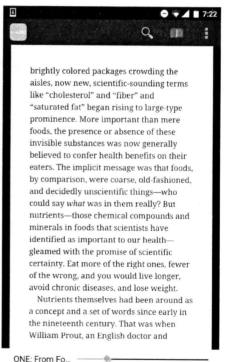

When you're on a page of text, clicking on the right side of the screen turns to the next page. Clicking on the left side goes back one page.

Click the bottom of the screen to bring up a menu of more options. This will show you where you are in the book.

If you want more options, click the three boxes at the top right:

From here you can change the look of the page on your screen. On mine, the default font was too large, and I was only able to read about two sentences at a time, so I reduced the font size to normal.

I also used the search function to find places where Pollan uses the words *industrial food*. If I click on any of these, I'll go directly to that page. This is a great tool when you're doing research and need to find where the author discussses specific concepts.

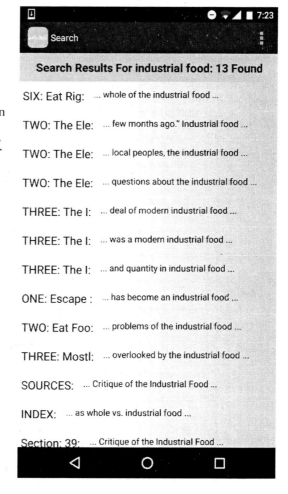

OVERDRIVE

On a computer or a phone (they're nearly identical)

Here's what it looks like when a book is offered electronically via Overdrive:

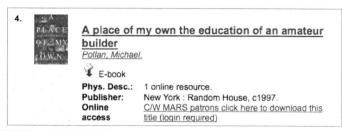

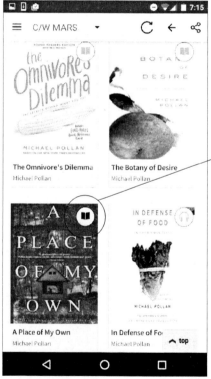

Note: In the upper right corner of each book is an icon. The symbol of the solid black book (over *A Place of My Own*) means the title is available.

The top two books are not (immediately) available—though you can place a hold on them and expect to be able to read them soon.

In Defense of Food is available (though not currently) as an audiobook.

If you're on a computer, you'll be prompted to download the Overdrive software. After doing so, here's what you'll see (it looks identical on both a computer and a phone).

If you download the file, it will expire in two weeks if you haven't already returned it.

I started reading the book on my computer, then switched to my phone. What's great about this software is that it knew where I had stopped reading and took me to that page when I moved to the phone. It also had the notes I'd made.

If you highlight a word, you'll be offered three options. ⟶

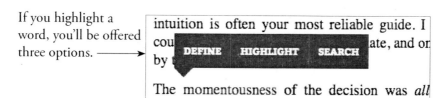

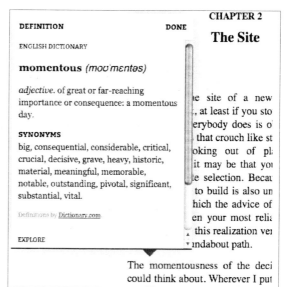

DEFINE

HIGHLIGHT

With this option, you can simply highlight the word, or you can add a note, as I did here.

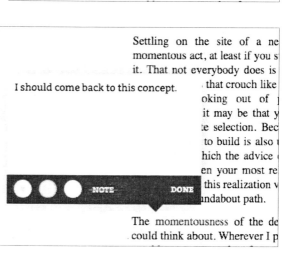

SEARCH

In this case, I searched for the word *prospect* because I knew it was an important concept in this book.

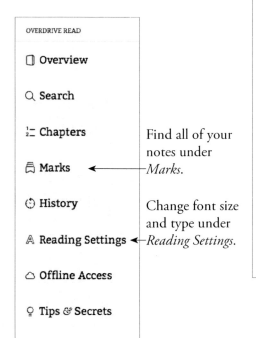

Find all of your notes under *Marks.*

Change font size and type under *Reading Settings.*

prospect

CHAPTER 1: A ROOM OF ONE'S OWN

1. ...hen I doubt there was anything I wanted to think about less. The **prospect** of embarking on any new construction project was so far out of t...

2. ...lf part—that I could not have foreseen. Judith suspects that the **prospect** of a house vibrating with the howls of an infant—our son, Isaac,...

CHAPTER 2: THE SITE

3. ...located according to the same principles. Vitruvius advises the **prospec**tive builder to seek a spot that is neither too high (where exposu...

4. ...thought long and hard about exactly what constituted a "pleasing **prospect**," as well as about the aesthetic and psychological experience of...

5. ...—seemed ideally suited to the project. They worked to make every **prospect** in their gardens look "natural." What they meant by this was tha...

6. ...for landscapes that offer a high degree of what Appleton calls **"prospect"** and "refuge": places that offer good views—of potential supplie...

7. ...ncidence that the type of landscape richest in opportunities for **prospect** and refuge is the savanna, where it is thought that the species...

The final word

Searching in the library catalog is becoming more and more like searching the Internet—but without all the pop-ups, viruses, broken links, etc. And with the increasing availability (and convenience) of electronic books, the library is more valuable than ever.

chapter 9

DATABASE RESEARCH

Knowing a great deal is not the same as being smart;
intelligence is not information alone but also judgment,
the manner in which information is collected and used.
    ~ Carl Sagan

Not long ago, college and university libraries were judged by their "holdings," i.e., how many books, journals, and other materials they owned. Students who attended big, prestigious universities had a distinct advantage over, say, community college students, because well-funded libraries had significantly bigger collections. If you wanted an article from the *Journal of Personality and Social Psychology* from the spring of 1966, you could probably find it at a big university—but not at a smaller college library.

By the 1980s, microfiche and microfilm allowed researchers to look at many more articles (magnified from tiny spools of film inside large, hot projector-like machines). These devices improved research for many students, but they were nowhere near as powerful as the one resource available to every college student today: *databases.*

Microfilm machine

These vast digitized storehouses hold more than *one hundred million* articles, images and other research materials.

Databases have everything from a recent *NPR* podcast (with transcript) on driverless cars . . .

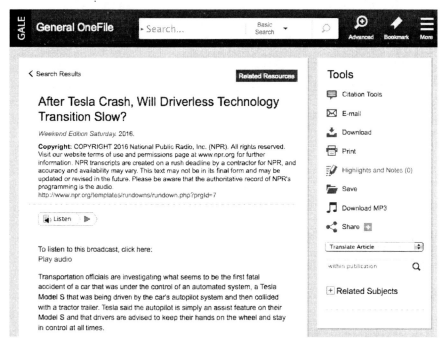

. . . to *New York Times* editorials from 1860 discussing the possibility of a Lincoln presidency.

Databases are an amazing storehouse of valuable research materials. Yet very few students take advantage of them, primarily because—at least compared to the Internet—databases are harder to find and more challenging to use, at least at first.

WHAT IS A DATABASE?

A database is a collection of articles (and other materials) from magazines, newspapers, encyclopedias, and scholarly journals. Some databases are general, like the one called "General OneFile," where I found that *NPR* piece. Others are more specialized, like the *New York Times* Historical database, where the Lincoln editorial came from. There are databases devoted to nursing, education, veterinary medicine, and many other fields. Generally, databases are available only by subscription; your college pays a considerable amount of money so that you can have access to these materials.

HOW DO YOU GET TO THE DATABASES?

Most college students will get to the databases via their college library's web page, which means first going to the college homepage. From there, the method of accessing the databases will vary. Below I demonstrate how it works at my college. If your college's site is confusing, ask a librarian for directions.

Go to your college's home page and click on **Library**.

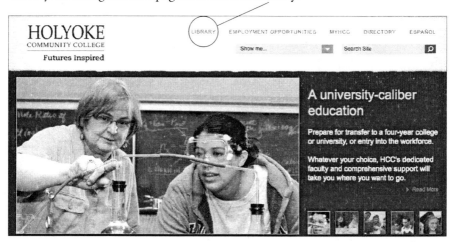

Switch to the tab marked **Databases.**

I recommend starting with *General Databases (Popular)*.

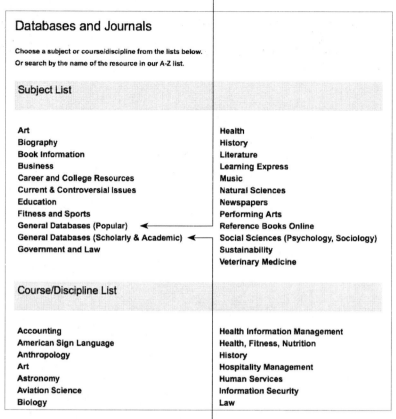

For more advanced research, try the *Scholarly & Academic* option.

Note also that you can search by course/discipline; this may be useful in future courses.

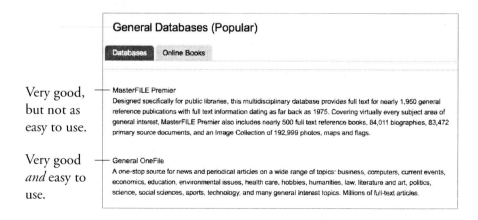

Here are most of the other databases available within the category of *General Databases*. All are useful for different purposes, of course. One that's not pictured here that many students like is Issues and Controversies. Scroll down further and you'll find it.

General Reference Center Gold
A general interest database that integrates a variety of sources - newspapers, reference books, magazines, and trade publications. Find articles on current events, popular culture, business and industry trends, the arts and sciences, sports, hobbies, and more.

Good for more basic research, . . .

Expanded Academic ASAP
Expanded Academic ASAP provides access to scholarly journals, magazines, and newspapers across disciplines. The database meets research needs in subject areas including the arts and humanities, social sciences, and science and technology.

for more advanced research, . . .

CQ Researcher
The CQ Researcher is an excellent source on the most critical events and controversial subjects of the day. Each of the 44 weekly issues offers a balanced, in-depth analysis of a contemporary topic by a veteran journalist, pro and con arguments by experts, a chronology, and annotated bibliographies to guide additional research. The CQ Researcher reports on important issues in a wide range of areas including social, economic, political, and environmental policy.

for current events and issues, . . .

Statista
Statista provides statistical data from thousands of institutions and sources. It provides access to data from market and opinion research institutions, as well as from business organizations and government agencies. Statista includes data on more than 85,000 topics from 18,000 sources. About 20 percent of the total data in Statista comes from sources available free online, such as the World Bank and the U.S. Census, but the data also includes numerous exclusive sources which include industry, marketing, and trade groups. Much of the data is related to marketing, demographic, government and industry information, and is international in scope. Data can be downloaded in JPG, PowerPoint and Excel.

⊘ Online Tutorial

for statistics, . . .

Films on Demand
Contains over 20,000 academic videos available for streaming. Watch full-length videos or one of over 231,000 video segments grouped by subject: Humanities & Social Sciences, Business & Economics, Science & Mathematics, Health & Medicine. Films on Demand also offers videos about careers.

for films and videos.

A BASIC DATABASE SEARCH

I'll begin with a simple search using General OneFile. The default search type is called "Basic," which is effectively a keyword search, much like Google.

To begin, I use the term *industrial food* in the search field. I tried a few different variations, such as adding the word *economy* (as I did in previous chapters), but this combination worked best. The lesson? Experiment.

However, even with good search terms, I didn't immediately get good results. As you can see from the titles below, these articles don't seem particularly useful.

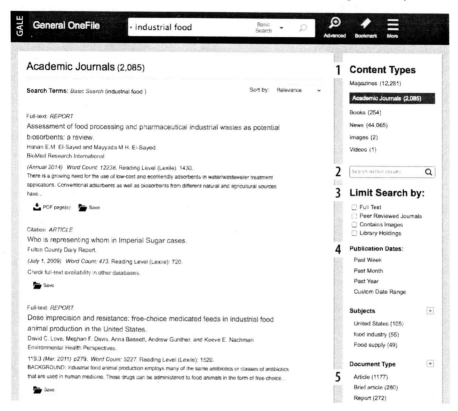

A few notes on some elements from the right-hand side of the screen above:

1 The system first shows you results from **academic journals**. This may be what you want, or you may want to change it to **magazines** if you're just getting started with your research or want material that's easier to read.

2 If you're getting too many results, add another search term here.

3 In most cases, you'll want to check the box marked "Full Text" under "Limit Search by." This way the database will only show you results you can actually read right now. If you're doing more advanced or specialized research, you may not want to check this box—that way, you can see all the results and then decide if you want to try to find them elsewhere.

4 If you only want recent research, limit your search here.

5 Often, limiting this to *Article* will give you better results.

TIP When you search in the databases, you have to work a little harder on your search terms than you do in Google. Make sure to use individual words that are important to your topic. If you include extra words (which you can get away with in Google), you typically won't get any results in database searches.

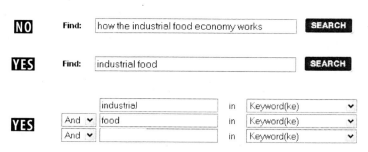

Even after doing the three things I suggest on the previous page, though, I was still getting mostly irrelevant results. So then I tried an advanced search like the one you can see in the box above this. Click here.

Then use the drop-down menu to switch to a keyword search.

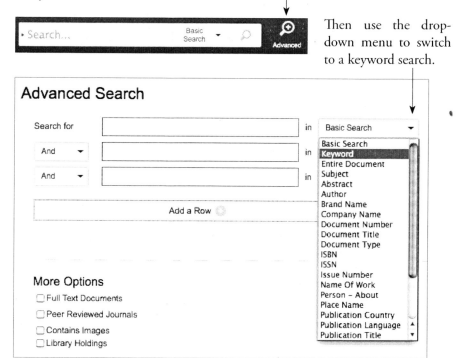

After getting the results from the advanced search, I switched from *Academic Journals* to *Magazines*. Again, most of the articles were about the food and/or restaurant industry. But I did find one article right away that looked promising.

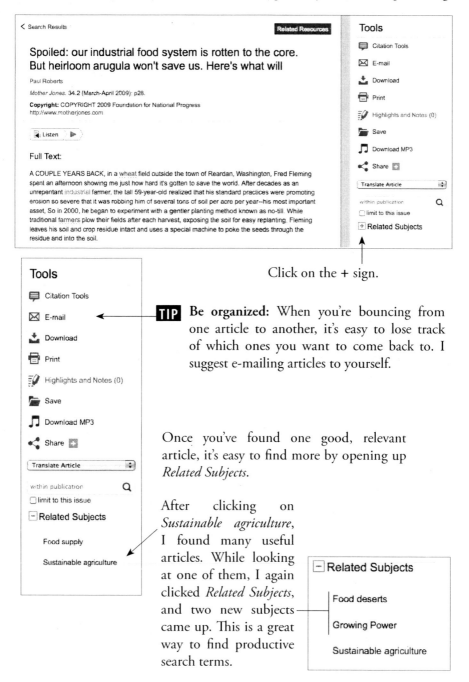

Click on the + sign.

TIP **Be organized:** When you're bouncing from one article to another, it's easy to lose track of which ones you want to come back to. I suggest e-mailing articles to yourself.

Once you've found one good, relevant article, it's easy to find more by opening up *Related Subjects*.

After clicking on *Sustainable agriculture*, I found many useful articles. While looking at one of them, I again clicked *Related Subjects*, and two new subjects came up. This is a great way to find productive search terms.

Content Types

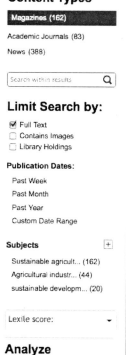

Magazines (162)

Academic Journals (83)

News (388)

Search within results 🔍

Limit Search by:

☑ Full Text
☐ Contains Images
☐ Library Holdings

Publication Dates:

Past Week

Past Month

Past Year

Custom Date Range

Subjects ➕

Sustainable agricult... (162)

Agricultural industr... (44)

sustainable developm... (20)

Lexile score: ▾

Analyze

◖ Topic Finder ◀

As you're looking at the search results, another useful tool is the Topic Finder. Below you can see the various topics generated on this wheel, and when you select one it shows more detailed information about that subject.

Topic Finder

There are two ways to visualize below which words and subjects are found most often in the text of your search results.

Visualization: ◉ Wheel ○ Tiles   Reset   Help

Topic Finder

There are two ways to visualize below which words and subjects are found most often in the text of your search results.

Visualization: ◉ Wheel ○ Tiles   Reset   Help

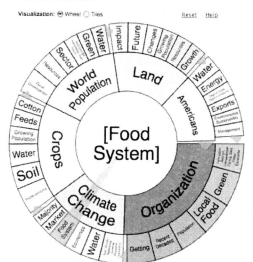

Results

Clicking on a topic wheel or tile narrows your original search results to the documents also containing that subject or term

Results for topic: **Food System** (6)

1. National Institute of Food and Agriculture

   Byline From USDA Agriculture Secretary Tom Vilsack launched the National Institute of Food and Agriculture NIFA with a major speech regarding the role of science and research at USDA At an event at the National Press. . [Agricultural industry] [Food safety] [Sustainable agriculture] [United States Department of Agriculture]

2. Governments rethinking locally grown concept

   Byline Jim Langcuster Auburn University The debate ensuing in Britain is also taking place a world away in the former British dominion of Australia It centers on one central question As farmers face the critical .. [Agricultural industry] [Government agencies] [Sustainable agriculture]

3. Kofi Annan 'I see the green revolution happening across Africa every day' with the right focus and sufficient political support, African agriculture can be a powerful

PEER-REVIEWED PUBLICATIONS

For some papers, you'll want to find legitimate scholarly materials: articles that have been published in academic journals that are *peer-reviewed*. When an article is peer-reviewed, it means that—before the article is published—other scholars have read the article and determined that it meets the standards of their field. For example, I was an editor for a peer-reviewed journal for a number of years. More than once, a peer reviewer read an article we were considering publishing and suggested that the writer familiarize herself with certain research that was relevant to her topic. In these cases, we wouldn't publish the article until the peer reviewer was satisfied with the quality of the research.

Although peer-reviewed articles are regarded as the most reliable and trustworthy sources available, it's worth remembering that peer review does not guarantee that the article will be true, or that there are not other legitimate ways of thinking about a subject.

Note: You can only check the option for peer-reviewed publications with academic journals and books; it doesn't apply to regular magazines.

Content Types

Academic Journals (1,358)

Books (5)

Search within results   Q

Limit Search by:

☑ Full Text
☑ Peer Reviewed Journals
☐ Contains Images
☐ Library Holdings

TIP When it comes to database searches, the single most important thing you can do is experiment. I've barely begun to describe what these databases can do—start clicking on things and find out. . . .

RESEARCHING CONTROVERSIAL ISSUES

I recommend *CQ Researcher* and *Opposing Viewpoints in Context* (you can find them both under the "General Databases").

The first one, *CQ Researcher*, offers lengthy articles introducing a range of compelling topics. For example, I simply used *technology* as a search term, and you can see some of the results on the next page.

CQ RESEARCHER
In-depth reports on today's issues

Help | Logout

Search by keyword...

Advanced Search

1923 - present

HOME   BROWSE TOPICS   BROWSE REPORTS   USING CQR   LIBRARIAN ACCOUNT   ABOUT

SEARCH RESULTS

Save this search | Create Topic Alert | Search content from CQ Press

1 - 25 of 31 results for **technology**   Show: 10 | **25** | 50   Sort by: Relevance | Newest | Oldest

Save to Favorites	Title	Date	Topic
☐	**Nanotechnology** . . . visitor at the Oxford Martin Programme on the Impacts of Future **Technology** at the University of Oxford. "The ramifications [will extend to] climate . . . View as PDF	6/10/2016	Consumer Protection and Product Liability
☐	**The Dark Web** . . . planet." (AP Photo/Niall Carson) Millions of people worldwide are using computer **technology** that allows them to visit websites, communicate with others and conduct . . View as PDF	1/15/2016	Currency
☐	**Robotics and the Economy** . . . the annual conference in October 2014 held by Gartner Inc., a **technology** research and advisory company, Research Director Peter Sondergaard said robots or . . . View as PDF	9/25/2015	Economic Analyses, Forecasts, and Statistics
☐	**Virtual Reality** . . . to treat phobias such as claustrophobia and acrophobia. (AFP/Getty Images/Boris Horvat) **Technology** that immerses users in artificial, but strikingly realistic, experiences is poised . . . View as PDF	2/26/2016	Popular Culture
☐	**Video Games and Learning** . . . all but a small fraction of children. The global spread of **technology** and migration of video games to mobile devices have helped propel . . . View as PDF	2/12/2016	Popular Culture

I read some of a number of these articles—all of them are quite long and thorough. It's worth remembering, though, that while these "articles" are well-researched, they are written by reporters, not by experts in these fields. Still, they are a good place to start your research and learn the basic positions and viewpoints surrounding a controversial issue.

Another database, *Opposing Viewpoints in Context*, has quite a few topics on its front page and can help you find a direction for your research. From the main page, I choose *Science, Technology and Ethics*, and the next page reveals more than forty additional subdivisions of that topic.

GALE

OPPOSING VIEWPOINTS

Opposing

Browse Issues   Maps   Curriculum Standards

Service members and their families face challenges with military life, including frequent moves and long deployments. **View More**

Business and Economics   View All

- Employment
- Government Spending
- Socialism

Energy and Environmentalism   View All

- Hybrid and Electric Cars
- Water Pollution
- Western US Droughts

Health and Medicine   View All

- Birth Defects
- Infectious Diseases
- Marijuana

Law and Politics   View All

- Capital Punishment
- Minimum Wage
- Self-Defense Laws

National Debate Topic   View All

- 2015-2016 National Debate Topic
- Espionage and Intelligence
- National Security

Science, Technology and Ethics   View All

- Animal Rights
- Social Media
- Technology and Society

Society and Culture   View All

- Body Image
- Civil Rights
- Same-Sex Marriage

War and Diplomacy   View All

- Domestic Terrorism
- Islamic State in Iraq and Syria (ISIS)
- Syria

Next, I choose *Technology and Education*, which takes me to the page below. It has a great variety of resources, including opinion essays, news reports, primary sources (see page 85), statistics, and links to articles from academic journals.

Technology and Education

2015 White House Science Fair

In the twentieth and twenty-first centuries, technology has increased worldwide and affected many aspects of human life. Some of the greatest applications of new technologies have been in the field of education. In countries throughout the world, schools began using computers, online programs, electronic devices, and other technological tools in lessons both in and out of classrooms. These technologies are meant to enhance student learning, allow students to interact in new ways, and develop skills needed in the modern world. While becoming increasingly common, use of technology in education remains controversial. Proponents of technology in education believe it essential for...View More

On This Page

- Featured Viewpoints 6
- Viewpoints 47
- Academic Journals 583
- Statistics 17
- Primary Sources 2
- Audio 76
- News 2,352
- Images 2
- Videos 11
- Reference 33
- Magazines 643
- Websites 8
- Related Topics

Featured Viewpoints 6

E-texts Provide Competition for Textbook Publishers

What Is the Role of Technology in Education?, 2013
From Opposing Viewpoints in Context

For Now, E-texts Will Not Disrupt the Textbook Industry

What Is the Role of Technology in Education?, 2013
From Opposing Viewpoints in Context

Free Internet-Based Education Can Change Education

What Is the Role of Technology in Education?, 2013
From Opposing Viewpoints in Context

Academic Journals 583

Reducing barriers to online access for people with...

Issues in Science and Technology, Winter 2011
From Opposing Viewpoints in Context

Assumptions and distance education

Distance Learning, January 2016
From Opposing Viewpoints in Context

A surging education sector

Distance Learning, January 2016
From Opposing Viewpoints in Context

Primary Sources 2

The future of higher education and how America will pay for...

The Future of Higher Education and How America Will Pay For It, June 2013
From Opposing Viewpoints in Context

The New Freedom Initiative

Social Policy: Essential Primary Sources, 2006
From Opposing Viewpoints in Context

Viewpoints 47

Motivating High School Students in Online Courses Is...

High School Alternative Programs, 2015
From Opposing Viewpoints in Context

Experts Have Diverse Predictions for the Future of Higher...

What Is the Future of Higher Education?, 2015
From Opposing Viewpoints in Context

The Online Challenge to Higher Education

What Is the Future of Higher Education?, 2015
From Opposing Viewpoints in Context

Statistics 17

Percentage of enrollments in distance education courses by...

Number of enrollments in distance education, by...

Number and percent of public school districts with students...

Audio 76

For Some Schools, Learning Doesn't Stop On Snow Days

All Things Considered, February 2, 2015
From Opposing Viewpoints in Context

The Online College That's Helping Undocumented Students

Morning Edition, October 26, 2015
From Opposing Viewpoints in Context

As Migrants Pour In, Germany Launches Online University For...

All Things Considered, October 16, 2015
From Opposing Viewpoints in Context

Search within page

Related Topics

Charter Schools

Education

For-Profit Education

More

chapter 10

MLA DOCUMENTATION

I want minimum information given with maximum politeness.
        ~ Jacqueline Kennedy

*The speed of communications is wondrous to behold. It is also true
that speed can multiply the distribution of information that we know
to be untrue.*
        ~ Edward R. Murrow

Why do your teachers care so much about documentation?

If you understand why documentation is important to academic work, you're
more likely to do it accurately in your papers—and avoid a charge of plagiarism.
Documenting your sources serves two purposes. First, it allows readers to know
which information or ideas belong to you and which are the product of your
research. Second, it enables readers to find those sources and examine them on
their own.

When do you need to document?

You need to document your source any time you use an idea or piece of
information that is not yours. If you don't document your sources properly, you
may be accused of plagiarism (see page 92).

When do you *not* need to document?

You don't need to cite "common knowledge," which includes strictly factual
information that can be found in a number of different sources. For example, if
you were writing a paper about Ireland and wanted to mention that the famine
happened between 1845 and 1850, you wouldn't need to document that fact
since it's widely available as a "fact" and not disputed. On the other hand, let's

say that you read an article in which the researcher asserted that the famine did not affect Ireland's Blasket Islands because the Islanders had a diet that was less reliant on potatoes. You *would* need to document this because the idea/assertion is not purely factual. The key difference is that the assertion about the Blasket Islanders is open to dispute or different interpretations. Anything that can be disputed or interpreted needs to be documented.

MLA, APA, Chicago, etc.—which one do you use?

It depends on what kind of paper you're writing because researchers in different fields follow different rules.

In English, for example, you use MLA (Modern Language Association), which is what this chapter covers. In psychology and other social sciences, you use APA (American Psychological Association), covered in Chapter 11. In history and other fields, it's Chicago. For most of the sciences, it's CSE (Council of Science Editors).

All four systems have some common features, so learning MLA should help you adapt to those other documentation styles.

MLA Documentation: a two-part process

Documenting your sources properly is a two-step process. Within your paper, you provide a brief reference to your source; this is called an in-text citation. At the end of the paper you provide complete information for all of your sources—this is the works-cited page.

MLA Documentation Directory

Books, continued

Internet and database sources

Other sources

Formatting

CITATIONS

Wh. .ay "in-text," I mean *your* text, the essay you're writing. For the examples here, pretend that these are sentences you would write in your paper. Pay attention to punctuation, spacing, and formatting.

In all of the sample sentences below, I have *integrated* the quoted or paraphrased material into my sentences. Make the material that you refer to a part of your sentence, and make sure that your sentence reads smoothly and is grammatically correct. Refer to pages 88-91 for additional guidelines.

BASIC RULES

I'll use a recent article from *The Atlantic* about robotics in medicine for the first few examples. Note that I found this article online (theatlantic.com), though I will also go over how it would look if you use the actual print version of the magazine.

Here's one part of the article that I want to use in my paper:

> Health care already represents one-sixth of America's gross domestic product. And that share is growing, placing an ever-larger strain on paychecks, corporate profits, and government resources. Figuring out how to manage this cost growth—how to meet the aging population's medical needs without bankrupting the country—has become the central economic-policy challenge of our time.

First, I put one of the ideas in my own words (see *paraphrasing* in Chapter 6):

Rising health care costs create a potential crisis for the American economy.

But this isn't my idea. *I* didn't come to this conclusion based on my research. The author of the article, Jonathan Cohn, did.

Important: No matter how you identify the "source" (usually the author), it must correspond with a works-cited entry. In other words, you must have a works-cited entry that begins **Cohn, Jonathan.**

There are two ways to give Cohn credit:

Method #1: Name the source in the sentence

This is the preferred method for citing a source. Use Jonathan Cohn's name in a signal phrase (see pages 87-88).

> **Jonathan Cohn argues that rising health care costs create a potential crisis for the American economy.**

Note: You only write the author's full name the first time you refer to him. After that, use only the author's last name: "Cohn argues that robots. . . ."

Method #2: Don't name the source in the sentence

If you don't name the source in your sentence via a signal phrase, you must do so in the parenthetical reference at the end of the sentence. Many professors prefer that students avoid this citation method; check with your professor.

> **Rising health care costs create a potential crisis for the American economy (Cohn).**

Using quotations

The two methods above work the same using a *direct quotation* (the writer's exact words, in his or her order):

> **Cohn observes that rising health care costs are "the central economic-policy challenge of our time."**

Or:

> **One commentator believes that rising health care costs are "the central economic-policy challenge of our time" (Cohn).**

Note: In the first example, the period goes *inside* the quotation marks. In the second example, the period goes after the parenthetical citation. Also, be sure to type a space after closing the quotation marks.

Using a source with page numbers

If your source is an actual book or magazine (or any other physical source with page numbers), you should include a page number in your citation. This is also the case if you're viewing a PDF that includes page numbers, which is frequently the case with scholarly articles.

I happen to subscribe to *The Atlantic*, and I also read this article in the magazine; the information I've been citing appeared on page 61, so my examples above would look like this:

> Jonathan Cohn argues that rising health care costs create a potential crisis for the American economy (61).

> Rising health care costs create a potential crisis for the American economy (Cohn 61).

> Cohn observes that rising health care costs are "the central economic-policy challenge of our time" (61).

> One commentator believes that rising health care costs are "the central economic-policy challenge of our time" (Cohn 61).

Note: There's no comma between the last name and the page number.

COMPLICATIONS TO THE BASIC RULES

Generally, the above examples will get you through the vast majority of in-text citations. But there's a good chance you'll have to deal with some variations.

Two authors

For the sake of simplicity, let's pretend that the article in *The Atlantic* was written by Cohn and a second author, James Gillen:

> Cohn and Gillen argue that rising health care costs create a potential crisis for the American economy.

Or:

> Rising health care costs create a potential crisis for the American economy (Cohn and Gillen).

Three or more authors

If there had been a third author, you only use the first author's name, followed by **et al.** (Latin for *and others*):

> Cohn et al. argue that rising health care costs create a potential crisis for the American economy.

Or:

> Rising health care costs create a potential crisis for the American economy (Cohn et al.).

With page numbers:

> Cohn et al. argue that rising health care costs create a potential crisis for the American economy (61).

> Rising health care costs create a potential crisis for the American economy (Cohn et al. 61).

No author listed

Pretend that the article in *The Atlantic* did not have an author listed; if you use a signal phrase, provide the full title of the article (but not a subtitle):

> In "The Robot Will See You Now," the author argues that rising health care costs are "the central economic-policy challenge of our time."

If you don't use a signal phrase, shorten the article title and put it in the parenthetical citation, inside quotation marks:

> One commentator believes that rising health care costs are "the central economic-policy challenge of our time" ("Robot").

If you used a source with page numbers:

> One commentator believes that rising health care costs are "the central economic-policy challenge of our time" ("Robot" 61).

Note: How you abbreviate the title is up to you, but be sure to use the first word that's not an article (a, an, the)—because this is the word a reader would be looking for on the works-cited page.

Quoting someone who's being quoted

This seems unusual, but it comes up often. In this example, I want to use part of the following quote, from the same article in *The Atlantic*.

> "We do now have robots performing surgery, but the robot is under constant supervision of the surgeon during the process," Baumol told a reporter from *The New York Times* two years ago. "You haven't saved labor. You have done other good things, but it isn't a way of cheapening the process."

Remember two things, and you'll get it right.

First, mention the person you're quoting (Baumol, in this case) in your sentence, and use his or her full name—which I had to find earlier in the article. Then, in your parenthetical reference, use the abbreviation *qtd. in* (for "quoted in") before the author of the article—because that's what your reader will be looking for on the works-cited page if she wants to find the article.

> **Economist William Baumol notes that the robots are "under constant supervision of the surgeon during the process" (qtd. in Cohn).**

Print version: If you read this in the print version of the magazine, your citation would be:

> **Economist William Baumol notes that the robots are "under constant supervision of the surgeon during the process" (qtd. in Cohn 66).**

Long quotation (also known as block quotation)

If you quote a passage that is four lines or longer, the first step is to mention the author's name in your sentence that preceeds the block quotation.

Your writing, to introduce the quotation.

> **By examining the marketing practices of mainstream grocery stores, Pollan reveals the preeminence of quantification:**

Block quotation, indented 1 inch from left. The right margin stays the same. It's double-spaced just like the rest of your text.

> > **Just look at the typical newspaper ad for a supermarket. The sole quality on display here is actually a quantity: tomatoes $0.69 a pound; ground chuck $1.09 a pound; eggs $0.99 a dozen—special this week. Is there any other category of product sold on such a reductive basis? (136)**

Your writing, to comment on the quotation.

> **By highlighting the focus on price and quantity, Pollan exposes a peculiar—and potentially dangerous—complicity between consumers and grocery businesses.**

Also note that the block quotation ends with the page number where you found the quotation, inside parentheses and *after* the punctuation mark. If your source has no page number, don't bother with the parenthetical reference. For help with formatting, see facing page.

Formatting a Block Quotation

If you quote a passage that is four or more lines long, format it as follows:

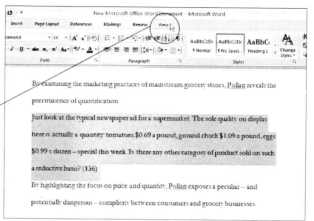

1. Start by highlighting the text you're quoting. Then, click on the **View** tab.

2. Check the **Ruler** box.

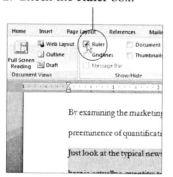

3. This little gadget is made up of three parts. You want to click on and hold the bottom one, the very small square, then drag it 1/2 inch to the right.

4. This is how it should look when you're finished.

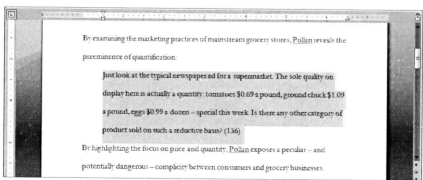

Changing the wording of quotations / Using brackets

Generally, you should quote your sources precisely, using their exact words. But sometimes you'll need to change a word or two for grammatical purposes, or remove part of a quotation. Let's say that I want to quote part of this sentence:

> The idea of robots performing surgery or more-routine medical tasks with less supervision is something many experts take seriously.

Just for the sake of this example, let's say that I want to restructure the quoted portion of the sentence, like this:

> **Cohn reports that if "robots [perform] surgery or more-routine medical tasks with less supervision," new concerns will arise.**

Because I'm no longer quoting Cohn word for word (*performing* has become *perform*), I have to indicate the alteration of the original wording by putting the word I've changed inside brackets.

Note: If I chose to use the word *performed*, though, I would only put the letters I changed inside brackets:

> **Cohn reports that if "robots perform[ed] surgery or more-routine medical tasks with less supervision," new concerns would arise.**

Using ellipses

If you remove a word or words from a quotation, use an ellipsis (three periods, with a space before and after each) to indicate the missing material:

> **Cohn notes that if "robots [perform] surgery . . . with less supervision," new concerns will arise.**

That's how you do it if you've removed a word or words from the middle of a sentence you're quoting.

If your quotation omits material from the end of a sentence, you *may* need to use an ellipsis. The rule is this: If your quoted material forms a complete sentence, but you're not quoting the entire sentence, use an ellipsis.

> All over the country, hospitals are on a hiring binge, desperate for people who can develop and install new information systems—and then manage them or train existing workers to do so.

Making the connection between information technology and medicine, Cohn writes, "All over the country, hospitals are on a hiring binge, desperate for people who can develop and install new information systems. . . ."

Finally, it gets slightly more complicated if you're quoting from multiple sentences and omitting some material. Here's another paragraph from the Cohn article, with the parts I plan to quote in bold:

> For the health-care system as a whole, **the efficiencies from the data revolution could amount to substantial savings.** One estimate, from the McKinsey Global Institute, suggested that the data revolution could yield onetime heath-care savings of up to $220 billion, followed by a slower rate of growth in health-care costs. Total health-care spending in the U.S. last year was $2.7 trillion, so that would be roughly the equivalent of reducing health-care spending by 7.5 percent up front. **That's the best reason to believe that the data revolution will make a difference,** even if it never lives up to the hype of its most enthusiastic proponents.

Here's one way to quote those elements:

Cohn believes that "the efficiencies from the data revolution could amount to substantial savings. . . . That's the best reason to believe that the data revolution will make a difference. . . ."

Note that I now have four dots—one to show the end of the first sentence, and then three more to make an ellipsis to indicate the missing material. If I had quoted all of the final sentence, I wouldn't have needed the second ellipsis.

One final complication. If I'm using the actual magazine as my source, I should include a page number. Here's what that would look like:

Cohn believes that "the efficiencies from the data revolution could amount to substantial savings. . . . That's the best reason to believe that the data revolution will make a difference . . ." (63).

Note how *one* of those four periods has moved to the very end of the sentence, after the page reference.

Work in an anthology

An anthology is a collection of essays, stories, or poems by many different authors. Many textbooks used in English courses are anthologies. For the in-text citation, you don't really need to worry about the fact that the book is an anthology. Just be sure that your citation refers to the actual writer of the story, poem or essay—not the editor(s) of the anthology.

> **Jane Smiley suggests that the problem may have its source in "the ubiquity of sugar" (328).**

Or:

> **Perhaps the problem is "the ubiquity of sugar" (Smiley 328).**

When you do the works-cited entry, you'll need to know the name of Smiley's essay, "Reflections on a Lettuce Wedge," the name of the anthology it appeared in, the name(s) of the anthology's editor(s), and other publication information. See pages 158-59 for more information.

Organization or group as author

This is tricky. First, you have to determine if the author and the publisher are the same. In the case of many organizations, they will be. If you're looking at a website, you generally want to scroll down to the bottom of any screen to find the publisher's name; it's usually next to the copyright symbol.

So, if the author and publisher are the same, you don't refer to an author in your sentence; instead, you use the title of whatever he or she wrote.

> *Foreign Languages and Higher Education: New Structures for a Changed World* **reports that as a result of various global conflicts, "Government language schools scrambled to redefine priorities and mount new programs."**

But you can also do it the other way, using a shortened version of the title:

> **As a result of various global conflicts, "Government language schools scrambled to redefine priorities and mount new programs"** (*Foreign Languages*).

Note: I did not include a page number for either citation because I found the quotation on the organization's website.

Author who wrote two or more books (that you cite in your paper)

Let's say that I read two books by Michael Pollan (*The Omnivore's Dilemma* and *In Defense of Food*), and I'm using them both as sources in my paper. So that there's no confusion about which book I'm referring to, I need to provide a shortened reference to the book inside the parentheses.

> **Michael Pollan asserts that both our civilization and our "food system" are "strictly organized on industrial lines" (*Omnivore* 201).**

Or:

> **It has been argued that both our civilization and our "food system" are "strictly organized on industrial lines" (Pollan, *Omnivore* 201).**

Note: If I had been using an article rather than a book, I would have still used a shortened form of the title, but it would be inside quotation marks, not italicized.

Two authors with same last name

It doesn't happen very often, but it does happen. If you refer to the author within the sentence, use the first and last name each time.

> **Christopher Alexander describes the problem this way: "A complex of buildings with no center is like a man without a head" (486).**

Or:

> **One architectural theorist describes the problem this way: "A complex of buildings with no center is like a man without a head" (C. Alexander 486).**

Two or more authors in the same sentence

Put the parenthetical citation immediately after the information you're citing from each author.

> **It has been said that heightened awareness of the sources of our food connects people to their "agricultural roots" (Smiley 437), or even to their "feral past" (Winckler 28).**

Two authors who make the same point

Again, this will happen only rarely. Your citation should name both authors, separated by a semi-colon.

> (Pollan 486; Jones 54).

Citing a Kindle, Nook, or other e-reader

If you were reading a physical book, you would cite the page number that you're quoting from. But because e-readers don't consistently have the same page numbering, you should *not* provide this information. Also, don't provide any other marker or indicator of location provided by the e-reader. However, if the book is divided into chapters (and you're confident that these would be the same in the physical book and in electronic versions), then do give the chapter.

> **Michael Pollan asserts that both our civilization and our "food system" are "strictly organized on industrial lines" (ch. 10).**

Or:

> **In Chapter 10, "Grass," Michael Pollan asserts that both our civilization and our "food system" are "strictly organized on industrial lines."**

Radio program / podcast / transcript

Treat these as you would any other source with an author. In this example, I listened to a podcast on NPR about companies sharing our online information. The author was listed as Brian Naylor. But I also consulted the written transcript to get the quotation. It doesn't matter which format I used here, but it will when I do the works-cited entry on page 170.

> **Brian Naylor asserts that these large companies "know more about you than you can imagine."**

Or, you may want to name the source—National Public Radio—specifically because it is widely viewed as a reliable source.

> **According to a National Public Radio report, these large companies "know more about you than you can imagine" (Naylor).**

WORKS-CITED ENTRIES

FIRST, A FEW UNIVERSAL GUIDELINES

The information on the next two pages is essential—don't skip past it. You'll need to come back to these basic guidelines as you write your works-cited entries.

Capitalization

It doesn't make much sense that you're supposed to capitalize titles "properly" when the journal or magazine article you're citing hasn't done so, but that's just how it is. Even if your source doesn't capitalize properly, you should.

So, even though a *Sports Illustrated* article appears as "Over The Top" in the database, you follow the rule that says not to capitalize articles ("the") and to write the title as "Over the Top."

Always capitalize	the first and last words of the title
	nouns, verbs, adjectives, and adverbs
Do *not* capitalize	prepositions: of, on, around, behind, and many more
	articles: a, an, the
	conjunctions: and, but, or, for, nor, so, yet
	infinitive: to

URLs

When citing a URL (web address), remove http:// or https://.

Long titles

Sometimes, particularly with newspaper and magazine articles, you'll come across some very long titles. Or at least they look that way; in many cases, what you're seeing is a headline and a sub-headline, as in this *New York Times* article:

The Trusted Grown-Ups Who Steal Millions From Youth Sports

Prosecutors in several states say embezzlement investigations involving youth sports have become common.

You have to use your judgment about what's really the title and what's not, but I do have a few suggestions. Use the whole title, even if it's long, when it's the title of a book or an article in a scholarly journal. Use a shortened version of the title when it's very, very long and/or the second part appears to be a complete sentence. Whenever possible, it helps to look at the original (or a PDF) so you can see the original formatting—then it's often obvious what the real title is.

Author names

The basic rule is that you reverse the order of the first author's name, but leave the others in the usual order.

One author: Smith, Doug K.

>   If Smith didn't have a middle initial: Smith, Doug.

Two authors: Smith, Doug K., and Walter T. White.

>   If Smith didn't have a middle initial: Smith, Doug, and Walter T. White.

Three or more authors: Smith, Doug K., et al.

>   If Smith didn't have a middle initial: Smith, Doug, et al.

>   (Et al. is an abbreviation for *and others*.)

Abbreviations of months

Most months are abbreviated; here's how all of them should look:

Jan.	**Feb.**	**Mar.**	**Apr.**
May	**June**	**July**	**Aug.**
Sept.	**Oct.**	**Nov.**	**Dec.**

Abbreviations of publishers' names

If the publisher is listed as, for example, The Macmillan Company, you would simply write Macmillan.

For academic journals, the publisher is often a university press. If, for example, it's Harvard University Press, you would abbreviate it Harvard UP or, for the University of Chicago Press, it would be U of Chicago P (no period—but my sentence now needs one).

Spaces

With some of the examples on the following pages, it's hard to tell where you should have a space. You always have a space after any mark of punctuation (comma, period, colon, semi-colon); also rememember that between each "part" of an entry (like, for example, between a magazine name and its date of publication), you always need a space.

The only exception to this rule is when you're using quotation marks, which come immediately after a comma or period, like "this," or "this."

Hanging indent

One of the unusual characteristics of the works-cited page is the "hanging indent." We do it this way because the Modern Language Association tells us to, but also because it makes sense. When you have quite a few works-cited entries, it's easier for the reader to find a particular source by browsing down the left side of the page (where all entries are alphabetized) to find the author name. You're much better off learning how to do it as I show on page 179 rather than using your tab key, which almost always results in weird formatting that's hard to fix.

Sample works-cited page

To see a properly formatted works-cited page, look at the sample student essay by Kyle Wright on pages 38-49.

HOW THE REST OF THIS CHAPTER IS ORGANIZED

• Books (below)

• Internet and database sources (pages 161-75)

• Other sources (pages 176-78)

Note: Because this book is intended to be a quick guide to the most common issues facing first-year writers, there are some sources that I'm not including here. If there's something I don't cover that you need to know how to cite, I recommend the Purdue University site, *The Owl at Purdue*.

BOOKS

On the next two pages, you can see where to find key information for documenting a book.

The spine, cover, and title page

The front cover

Here you should find the full title, though sometimes there's so much additional information on the cover that it can be hard to tell exactly what the title is. When there's a subtitle, it's even more confusing. Looking at the title page can help.

The title page

Title, subtitle, author, publisher, and year of publication—all on one page. (It's not always this straightforward.)

Note: Everything here is capitalized, which you do not want to do in your documentation. See specific guidelines on capitalization on page 151.

The spine

The spine (or edge) of the book will usually have the full name of the book (often with subtitle, as in this case) and the author's full name. The spine is also the most reliable place to find the name of the publisher; this case is unusual in that it shows a penguin rather than the name of the publisher, which happens to be . . . Penguin Books.

The copyright page

If the title page doesn't list the year of publication, here's where you'll need to look. There's a lot of information on this page, but just find the © symbol. If you find a number of different years on this page, use the most recent one.

THE PENGUIN PRESS
Published by the Penguin Group
Penguin Group (USA) Inc., 375 Hudson Street, New York, New York 10014, U.S.A. •
Penguin Group (Canada), 90 Eglinton Avenue East, Suite 700, Toronto, Ontario, Canada
M4P 2Y3 (a division of Pearson Penguin Canada Inc.) • Penguin Books Ltd, 80 Strand,
London WC2R 0RL, England • Penguin Ireland, 25 St. Stephen's Green, Dublin 2,
Ireland (a division of Penguin Books Ltd) • Penguin Books Australia Ltd, 250
Camberwell Road, Camberwell, Victoria 3124, Australia (a division of Pearson Australia
Group Pty Ltd) • Penguin Books India Pvt Ltd, 11 Community Centre, Panchsheel Park,
New Delhi – 110 017, India • Penguin Group (NZ), Cnr Airborne and Rosedale Roads,
Albany, Auckland 1310, New Zealand (a division of Pearson New Zealand Ltd) •
Penguin Books (South Africa) (Pty) Ltd, 24 Sturdee Avenue,
Rosebank, Johannesburg 2196, South Africa

Penguin Books Ltd, Registered Offices: 80 Strand, London WC2R 0RL, England

First published in 2006 by The Penguin Press
a member of Penguin Group (USA) Inc.

Copyright © Michael Pollan, 2006 ◄— The year of publication
All rights reserved   appears after the © symbol.

LIBRARY OF CONGRESS CATALOGING IN PUBLICATION DATA
Pollan, Michael.
The omnivore's dilemma : a natural history of four meals / Michael Pollan.
p.   cm.
Includes bibliographical references and index.
ISBN 1-59420-082-3
1. GT2850 .P65 2006.   2. Food habits.   3. Food preferences.   I. Title.
GT2850.P65 2006
394.1'2—dc22   2005056557

Printed in the United States of America

13   15   17   19   20   18   16   14

DESIGNED BY MARYSARAH QUINN

Book with one author

> Author's Last Name, First Name. *Book Title: Book Subtitle**. Publisher, Year of Publication.

* Include subtitle after a colon, and always capitalize the first word after the colon.

> Pollan, Michael. *The Omnivore's Dilemma: A Natural History of Four Meals*. Penguin, 2006.

Book with two, three, or more authors

See guidelines on page 152 for how to write additional author names.

Kindle, Nook, iPad, or e-book

If you read the book on a Kindle, Nook, iPad, or similar device, you don't need to add anything to your entry.

However, if you read an e-book online, you should include information about the name of the site where you viewed it (an app called OverDrive, in this case), and the URL, if available:

> Shteyngart, Gary. *Super Sad True Love Story*. Random House, 2010. *OverDrive*, ofs-650f28f6a35e6f81781172bfd6f72d78.read.overdrive. com/?p=PKb5cZSEUrd5abAgh1yKwg.

Book with an editor

The editor is listed as the "main" author for the sake of the works-cited entry. Keep in mind, though, that if you cite particular essays or stories from within this book, you need an entry for each of these authors too. Yes, this is a little confusing. See also the guideline for *Work in an anthology* on page 158.

As far as the works-cited entry goes, this is just like any other book, with the simple addition of the word editor(s).

> Hofstadter, Albert, and Richard Kuhns, editors. *Philosophies of Art and Beauty: Selected Readings in Aesthetics from Plato to Heidegger*. U of Chicago P, 1964.

Book that lists an edition

Many books (textbooks, especially) are republished with the same title but new content. If your book has an edition listed, it will probably be noticeable on the cover and/or the spine. In the works-cited entry, put the edition after the title.

> McQuade, Donald, and Robert Atwan, editors. *The Writer's Presence: A Pool of Readings.* 5th ed., Bedford / St. Martin's, 2007.

Two or more books by same author

Use three hyphens to indicate a repeat of the author's name. Put each book in alphabetical order (*In* before *Omnivore*).

> Pollan, Michael. *In Defense of Food: An Eater's Manifesto.* Penguin, 2008.

> ---. *The Omnivore's Dilemma: A Natural History of Four Meals.* Penguin, 2006.

Book by an anonymous author

Don't write Anonymous or Anon. for the author. Just go straight to the title.

> *Primary Colors: A Novel of Politics.* Random House, 2006.

Book by an organization or group

If the author and the publisher are the same, start with the book title.

> *MLA Style Manual and Guide to Scholarly Publishing.* 8th ed., Modern Language Association of America, 2016.

Book that has been translated

Start with the person who wrote the book, *not* the translator.

> Barthes, Roland. *The Eiffel Tower and Other Mythologies.* Translated by Richard Howard, Noonday, 1979.

Book in more than one volume

After the title, write the volume number that you used.

Kelby, Scott. *The Digital Photography Book*. Vol. 2, Peachpit Press, 2008.

Book that has a title within the title

When scholars write about another book, they often include the title of the book in *their* title. Don't italicize the title that appears within their title.

Brodhead, Richard H., editor. *New Essays on* Moby-Dick. Cambride UP, 1986.

Work in an anthology—a book with many different authors

Many textbooks, particularly in English classes, are *anthologies*; an anthology is a collection of works (essays, stories, poems, and/or plays) written by many different authors. If you're using one essay from an anthology, here's how you cite it:

Author's Last Name, First Name. "Title of Essay." *Name of Book,* edited
by First Name Last Name, edition, Publisher, Year of Publication,
page range.

Hughes, Langston. "Salvation." *The Writer's Presence: A Pool of Readings,*
edited by Donald McQuade and Robert Atwan, 5th ed., Bedford /
St. Martin's, 2007, pp. 163-65.

This is correct; it should *not* be 163-165.

- This is the guideline for when you're citing only one essay, story, play, or poem from an anthology; if you cite more than one, see the next entry.
- The editors' names will be on the front of the book and on the title page.

Two or more works from the same anthology

When you use two different authors from the same anthology, you use what the MLA calls a "cross-reference." Do a shortened entry for each essay, story, or poem, and also do a full entry for the whole book.

Note: Put each entry on your works-cited page wherever it belongs alphabetically; in other words, these would not necessarily be grouped together.

Entry for individual essay you read in the anthology

Hughes, Langston. "Salvation." McQuade and Atwan, pp. 163-65.

Full entry for whole book

McQuade, Donald, and Robert Atwan, editors. *The Writer's Presence: A Pool of Readings*, 5th ed., Bedford / St. Martin's, 2007.

Entry for individual essay you read in the anthology

Wolfe, Tom. "Hooking Up." McQuade and Atwan, pp. 611-18.

This is correct; it should *not* be 611-618.

Work in a professor's "course packet" or handout

Ideally, your professor has provided citation information for the source, in which case you should use his or her citation. If not, start with the author and title of the work you're citing, followed by the most logical information about the course packet you can find. If the professor has titled the course packet, use that as the title and name him as the person who "compiled" the selections, followed by information about the course.

> Author's Last Name, First Name. "Title of Essay." *Title of Course Packet,* compiled by First Name Last Name, course handout, Name of Course and Course Number, Name of College, Semester and Year, page range.

> Saunders, George. "Escape from Spiderhead." *The Persistence of Reality: Readings*, compiled by James Dutcher, course handout, English 230, Holyoke Community College, Fall 2015, pp. 163-65.

If the course packet has no title, use the following guideline:

> Saunders, George. "Escape from Spiderhead." Course handout, compiled by James Dutcher and Ileana Vasu, Honors 206, Holyoke Community College, Fall 2015, pp. 389-98.

Comic book

For a comic book, you should identify the title of the particular issue you're using, followed by the title of the series.

> Author's Last Name, First Name. *Title of Issue. Title of Series,* issue number, Publisher, Year of Publication.

> Lemire, Jeff. *Machine Moon. Descender,* no. 2, Image Comics, 2016.

To be slightly more accurate, you may also want to include the name of the artist:

> Lemire, Jeff. *Machine Moon.* **Illustrated by Dustin Nguyen.** *Descender,* no. 2, Image Comics, 2016.

Graphic novel

This citation is identical to any other book; see page 156. If you need to add the name of an illustrator, see the example just above this one.

Encyclopedia or dictionary

In most reference books (such as encyclopedias and dictionaries), no author is listed, so you simply start with the title of the entry. After the name of the book, include the edition (abbreviated as below) and the year. If there *is* an author listed, then put that first. But I have a feeling you knew that.

> "Botox." *The New Encyclopædia Britannica.* 15th ed. 2003.

Book that you read online

> Author's Last Name, First Name. *Book Title: Book Subtitle.* Publisher, Year of Publication. *Name of Site,* URL.

> Orejan, Jaime. *Football / Soccer: History and Tactics.* McFarland, 2011. *Google Books,* books.Google.com/books?id=H0l2T7tLSiEC&lpg= PP1&dq=soccer%20football&pg=PR4#v=onepage&q=soccer%20 football&f=false.

INTERNET AND DATABASE SOURCES

For many of you, this is where you'll find most of your sources, which is why I'm illustrating these guidelines more prominently.

Article you found online

This is the guideline you'd use for just about any "article" you find online. There's an additional—slightly more complex—example on the next two pages.

Author's Last Name, First Name. "Title of Article: Subtitle." *Name of website*, Date, URL.

Cohn, Jonathan. "The Robot Will See You Now." *The Atlantic*, 20 Feb. 2013, www.theatlantic.com/magazine/archive/2013/03/the-robot-will-see-you-now/309216/.

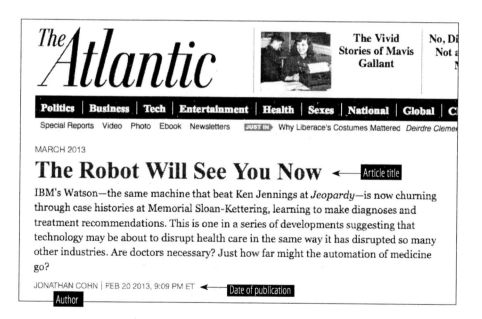

- Generally, you should not include subtitles for magazine articles (see guidelines for long titles on page 151).

- If the article has no author listed, simply start your entry with the title of the article (inside quotation marks). See page 169 for more information.

Article you found online, with complications

This is the same guideline as on the previous page, but it has some additional elements that make it slightly more complicated. See facing page.

> Author's Last Name, First Name. "Title of Article: Subtitle." *Name of website*, Date, URL.

> Quart, Alissa. "'Middle Class' Used to Denote Comfort and Security. Not Anymore." *The Guardian*, 7 July 2016, www.theguardian. com/commentisfree/2016/jul/07/middle-class-struggle-technology-overtaking-jobs-security-cost-of-living.

This is an unusual title for a couple of reasons:

First, it has quotation marks around the first two words, which means you need to use single quotation marks, 'like this,' around those words. But your entire title needs to have standard quotation marks, "like this."

Second, the title includes a period and a second "sentence." It's not exactly a sentence, but it's definitely part of the title. So you should include it, with the period. In many cases, though, you would not want to include an additional sentence that appears after the title. Again, you have to use your judgment and common sense. See more about long titles on page 151.

Comment on an article

Begin with the screen name of the person who wrote the comment. Use the date the comment was made—in this case, "3d ago" (three days ago), which was the day of publication. If an exact time is provided, add it; for the sake of this example, let's pretend it was 9:18 p.m. If possible, include a URL that will go directly to the comment, as I do here.

> eminijunkie 3d ago   9 ↑
>
> Middle class still denotes comfort and security. It's not that it no longer does that, just that a lot of people who think they are middle class are no longer middle class.

> Eminijunkie. Comment on "'Middle Class' Used to Denote Comfort and Security. Not Anymore." *The Guardian*, 7 July 2016, 9:18 p.m., www.theguardian.com/commentisfree/2016/jul/07/middle-class-struggle-technology-overtaking-jobs-security-cost-of-living#comment-78441867.

theguardian

home › opinion | election 2016 | US | world | sports | soccer· | tech | arts | lifestyle ≡ all

Society
Opinion

'Middle class' used to denote comfort and security. Not anymore

Article title

Alissa Quart ← Author

The apps and robots celebrated by Silicon Valley wunderkinds are helping make previously white-collar lives ever more precarious

Sub-headline (not part of title)

McDonald's workers aren't the only employees who deserve fair, steady hours. Adjunct professors do, too.
Photograph: John Lund/Drew Kelly/Getty Images/Blend Images

Thursday 7 July 2016 07.15 EDT ← Date of publication

Shares   Comments
164   123

Precariousness is not just a working-class thing. In recent interviews, dozens of academics and schoolteachers, administrators, librarians, journalists and even coders have told me they too are falling prey to an unstable new America. I've started to think of this just-scraping-by group as the Middle Precariat.

Article (not scholarly) in a database

These articles typically appear in magazines geared toward the general public rather than scholars in a field.

Author's Last Name, First Name. "Title of Article: Subtitle." *Name of Publication,* date, page range. *Name of Database,* URL.

Cohn, Jonathan. "The Robot Will See You Now." *The Atlantic,* Mar. 2013, pp. 58-69. *General OneFile.*

- The guideline calls for a "page range," but the database doesn't provide this information—it only gives the starting page. In this case, use that page and the + symbol, so it looks like this: pp. 58+. Or, if you want to be thorough, look at the PDF, which is where I saw that the article ended on p. 69.

- The capitalization shown for the article title needs to be corrected (see guidelines on page 151).

- About the URL: MLA says that you should usually include it, but it does say that this is at the discretion of the professor. I don't think most professors would want it included in this case for two good reasons. First, it was extremely long (almost 7 lines); second, the URL would only work in the HCC database.

Article (scholarly) in a database

These articles appear in academic journals, many of which are peer-reviewed (see pages 16 & 132). They are typically written for other scholars in the field.

Author's Last Name, First Name. "Title of Article: Subtitle." *Name of Publication,* vol. X, no. X, date: page range. *Name of Database,* URL or doi.

Kac, Eduardo. "Foundation and Development of Robotic Art." *Art Journal,* vol. 56, no. 3, Autumn 1997, pp. 60-67. *JSTOR,* doi:10.2307/777838

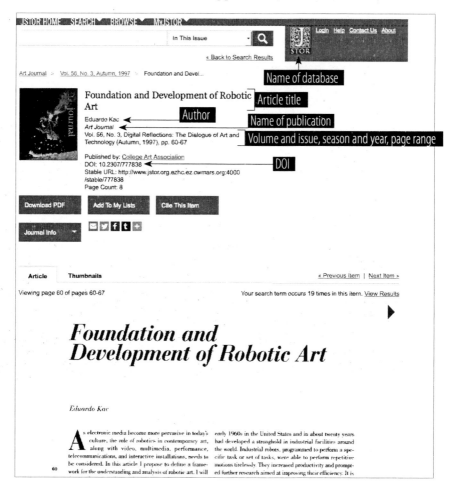

- If the DOI (digital object identifier) is available, use it. Second best is a "stable" URL (one that is unlikely to change), which is also available for this article. Third best is a regular URL.

Blog post

You'll notice that this is almost exactly like the format for any online article. The only real difference is that on many blogs, writers don't use their full names—or they use a pseudonym. Whatever name the person uses is the one you should use for your works-cited entry.

Author. "Title of Blog Post." *Name of website*, date, URL.

Petra. "Unity and Nihilism in *Game of Thrones* and *A Song of Ice and Fire*." *Watchers on the Wall*, 11 July 2016, watchersonthewall.com/unity-nihilism-game-thrones-song-ice-fire/.

As of the end of season 6, *Game of Thrones* and *A Song of Ice and Fire* (ASOIAF) have truly gone their separate ways. Plot lines and character arcs have taken drastically different trajectories, and, as the two series continue to diverge, the points of comparison between them become more prominent, not only in terms of story but also in terms of theme and character development.

Note that I added italics to the titles of the TV show and the book. It's the same principle that tells us to fix the capitalization of titles.

Document published by government agency

If you're using an entire publication, as in the case below, this is the appropriate guideline. If you're using a web page published by an organization (including a government organization), use the guideline on the next page.

Start by providing the name of the government—in the U.S., this will typically be either United States or the name of a state—followed by the name of the agency that published the document. You may also need to list a "sub-agency." Note: I found the reference to the Department of Education at the bottom of the page.

Government, Agency, Sub-Agency [if needed]. *Name of Publication*, date, URL.

United States, Department of Education, National Center for Education Statistics. *The Condition of Education*, 2016, nces.ed.gov/programs/coe/.

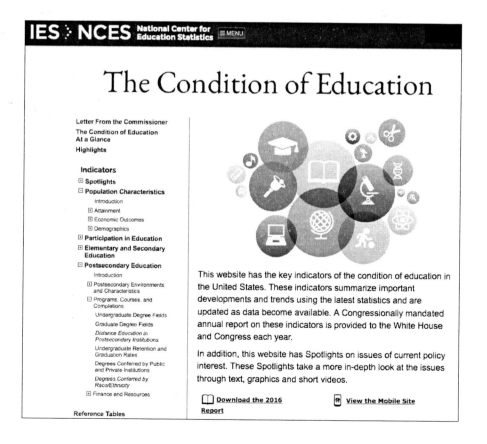

Online page published by government agency or an organization

In many cases, the author is the same as the publisher. When that's the case, you don't list an author—go straight to the title of the article.

"Title of Article." *Name of website*, publisher, date, URL. Accessed date.

"Foreign Languages and Higher Education: New Structures for a Changed World." *MLA*, Modern Language Association of America, www.mla.org/Resources/Research/Surveys-Reports-and-Other-Documents/Teaching-Enrollments-and-Programs/Foreign-Languages-and-Higher-Education-New-Structures-for-a-Changed-World. Accessed 6 July 2016.

- I didn't include a date in my entry because there was none listed. If there's no date, you should provide information about when you found the source, as I do after the URL above. If the article does include a date, put it after the publisher, before the URL.

If you use a library database for research, you'll find that many of the databases offer a "citation generator." This can save you some time if you

have a number of database sources, but be sure to check the entries—they often have mistakes. I offer the same caution about using services such as EasyBib and Citation Machine. They generally work well if you put in the correct information, but it's still smart to check for errors.

Article with no author

As with many "news" stories online, there's no author listed for this article. Start with the article title and proceed as you would with other online entries: name of webpage, date, URL.

"911 Caller: Husband Won't Eat Dinner." *NBC News*, 24 Dec. 2009,

www.nbcnews.com/id/34577354/ns/us_news-weird_news/t/caller-

husband-wont-eat-dinner/#.V4UcCa7fIUM.

Twitter

Start with the writer's screen name, followed by actual name (if provided) in parentheses, followed by the entire Tweet, inside quotation marks—you *don't* need to correct the capitalization—but do capitalize the first word. Include hashtags if they're part of the Tweet.

@eyeballhatred (Clay Banes). "Life is like a tree / in the men's room

/ at Auto Express in Hadley, MA. @ Auto Express Hadley."

25 June 2016, 10:02 a.m. *Twitter*, twitter.com/eyeballhatred/

status/746750462892793856

Podcast / radio program

Let's say that you heard a program on NPR (National Public Radio) that you want to use in your paper; find it online and consider a couple of questions before you decide how to document it. If it looks like the example below—with a clearly listed author and the text of podcast, which was read on the radio—this is pretty simple.

If you can't find an author's name, move to the next example.

Author's Last Name, First Name. "Title of Podcast / Article." *Name of website,* date, URL. Transcript.

Naylor, Brian. "Firms Are Buying, Sharing Your Online Info. What Can You Do About It?" *National Public Radio,* 11 July 2016, www.npr.org/sections/alltechconsidered/2016/07/11/485571291/firms-are-buying-sharing-your-online-info-what-can-you-do-about-it. Transcript.

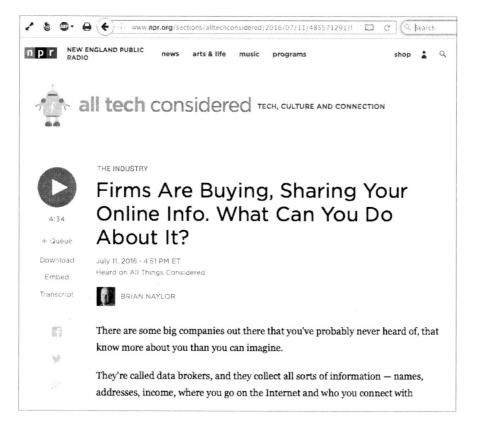

Podcast / radio program, with complications

As I was browsing the NPR site, I came across a podcast called "The Stink Tree." I wanted to demonstrate how to document a podcast that has no transcript and no author listed. Here's the easy (some might say lazy) way to document this source.

"The Stink Tree." *National Public Radio,* 27 May 2016, www.npr.org/ podcasts/510303/how-to-do-everything.

One problem is that I wasn't sure the link would bring a reader directly to that specific podcast. It also bothered me that I couldn't figure out who the authors of the podcast were. There's just not much information here:

So I went back to the top of the page and clicked on this link.

There, I was able to see a little more information and get a URL that would go directly to the podcast. But the key piece of the puzzle was finding the "About Our Show" link.

Using the new information, here's what I came up with:

Danforth, Mike, and Ian Chillag. "The Stink Tree." *How To Do Everything,* 27 May 2016, howtodoeverything.org/post/145026822225/this-week- we-save-a-marriage-and-improve-the-most#tumblr_notes.

What's interesting is how different this citation is from the one at the top of the page. I think both are acceptable, but this one is more specific. The point is this: With MLA documentation, there's not always a single right way to do a citation. You have to use some judgment—and often investigate further.

YouTube / Vimeo / Online video

These are generally like online articles, though it can be challenging to find an author. Open the "Show More" box to get that and other information.

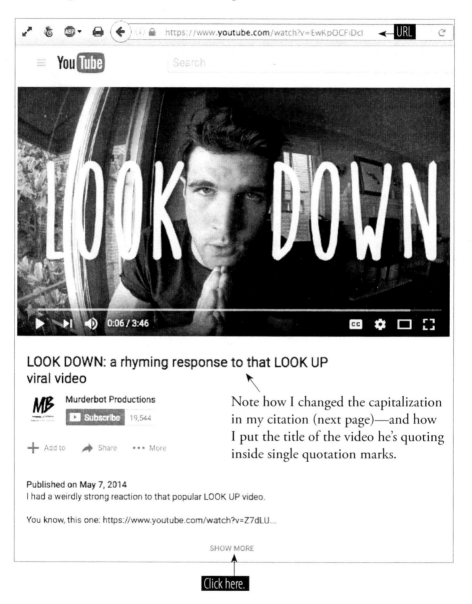

LOOK DOWN: a rhyming response to that LOOK UP viral video

Note how I changed the capitalization in my citation (next page)—and how I put the title of the video he's quoting inside single quotation marks.

YouTube / Vimeo / Online video (continued)

Author Last Name, First Name. "Title of Video: Subtitle." *Name of website,*
    date, URL.

Sleeper, Jarrett. "Look Down: A Rhyming Response to That 'Look
    Up' Viral Video." *YouTube*, 7 May 2014, www.youtube.com/
    watch?v=EwKpOCFiDcI.

In this case, I had to make a judgment call about the author's name. I assume
it's a pseudonym, so I Googled the name provided here, Jarrett Sleeper, and I
found a number of links connected to that name. On that basis, I thought it was
appropriate to use it.

Online video / TEDTalks

This is similar to the previous example but slightly more complicated.

Online video / TEDTalks (continued)

Author Last Name, First Name. "Title of Video: Subtitle." *Name of Organization Hosting the Talk / Video,* date of publication. *Name of website,* date, URL.

Turkle, Sherry. "Connected, but Alone?" *TedTalks,* 3 Apr. 2012. *YouTube,* www.youtube.com/watch?v=t7Xr3AsBEK4.

This is another case where you have to use some common sense. What looks like the title of the video, "Sherry Turkle: Connected, but alone?" contains both the name of the author and the title of her talk. That's easy to figure out once you start watching some of the video—in the photograph, you can see Ms. Turkle and her name, and she introduces herself. So it makes sense to list her as the author.

Note also how I corrected the capitalization of the title.

Another piece of information that could be useful to your reader is the name of the organization that's hosting Turkle's talk: TEDTalks. As you can see from the citation above, that goes in italics and is followed by the information about where you watched the video: YouTube.

OTHER SOURCES

Film / DVD (of a movie, not a TV show)

> *Title of Film.* Directed by First Name Last Name, Name of Studio that
> produced film, Year of release.

> *Inglourious Basterds.* Directed by Quentin Tarantino, Universal Pictures,
> 2009.

If your essay focuses more on the director, reorder the entry as follows, noting
changes in punctuation:

> Tarantino, Quentin, director. *Inglourious Basterds.* Universal Pictures,
> 2009.

If you watched the movie online, add information about the site where you
viewed it, along with the URL.

> *Inglourious Basterds.* Directed by Quentin Tarantino, Universal Pictures,
> 2009. *Amazon,* www.amazon.com/Inglourious-Basterds-Brad-Pitt/
> dp/B002YCVX5S.

Television show

Basic entry:

> "Title of Episode." *Title of Show,* created by First Name Last Name,
> season X, episode X, *Publisher,* date show aired or was released.

> "We'll Always Have Baltimore." *Orange Is the New Black,* created by
> Jenji Kohan, season 4, episode 5, *Netflix,* 17 June 2016.

The above is slightly unusual because the show was produced by Netflix. In many
other cases, you'd have the name of the network (HBO, CBS, etc.) in that spot.
Also, you can typically check Wikipedia to find the name of any show's creator.

If you watch the show somewhere other than where it originally appeared, you
should include that information. I use Hulu in these examples and included a
URL. If you use Netflix, you won't have a URL.

"Title of Episode." *Title of Show*, created by First Name Last Name, season X, episode X, *Publisher*, date show aired or was released. *Site where you viewed episode*, URL.

"Buckle Up." *Scandal*, created by Shonda Rhimes, season 5, episode 19, *ABC*, 28 Apr. 2016. *Hulu*, www.hulu.com/watch/935545.

If you're focusing on the work of the director, you can name her as well:

"Buckle Up." *Scandal*, created by Shonda Rhimes, directed by Regina King, season 5, episode 19, *ABC*, 28 Apr. 2016. *Hulu*, www.hulu.com/watch/935545.

If you're focusing on the acting, you might name the actor:

"Buckle Up." *Scandal*, performance by Kerry Washington, season 5, episode 19, *ABC*, 28 Apr. 2016. *Hulu*, www.hulu.com/watch/935545.

If you watched it on DVD, just be sure to get the title right; in this case, it's slightly different. Also, you remove the season number. Finally, if there are multiple discs, indicate which disc the episode is on with a comma and disc X after the date.

"Buckle Up." *Scandal: The Complete Fifth Season*, created by Shonda Rhimes, episode 19, 2016.

Image / Photograph / Artwork

If the image is part of a collection in a gallery or a museum, document it as follows:

Artist's Last Name, First Name. *Title of artwork*. Year the artwork was produced, Museum or Gallery where it is found, City of Museum/Gallery. *Name of website*, URL.

Giacometti, Alberto. *Man Pointing*. 1947, Tate Gallery, London. *Tate*, www.tate.org.uk/art/artworks/giacometti-man-pointing-n05939.

If you viewed the artwork in person rather than online, don't include the name of the website or the URL.

If the artwork does not appear to be part of a museum or gallery collection—if, for example, it only exists online—then format it as follows, more like a standard web page.

> **Name of artist. "Title of artwork."** *website name*, **year the artwork was produced, URL.**

> **Thayer, Tim. "Robot England."** *OtterJet*, **2015, otterjet.com/works/ robot-england/.**

E-mail message

> **Last Name, First Name (of person who wrote email). "Subject of Message." Received by Your Name (or name of person who received the message, if not you), date of e-mail.**

> **Shirk, Zoe. "Re: Further Thoughts on Writing Process." Received by Fred Cooksey, 25 June 2016.**

If the subject line isn't properly capitalized, fix it. In this case, pretend that the subject actually appeared as "Re: further thoughts on writing process."

Interview

> **Last Name, First Name (of person you interviewed). Personal interview, date of interview.**

> **Gillen, Claire. Personal interview, 4 July 2016.**

Formatting a Hanging Indent

1. Start by highlighting all of your works cited entries. (It's best to do this when you're finished typing all the entries—I'm only doing one here.) Then, click on the **View** tab.

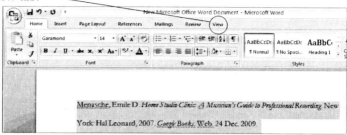

2. Check the **Ruler** box.

3. Now that you can see the ruler, you want to find the little gadget on the left that determines your indentation. It's made up of three parts. You want to click on and hold the triangular one in the middle, then drag it 1/2 inch to the right.

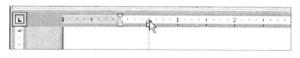

Note: If you let your cursor hover over the boxes, it will display the function; when it says **Hanging Indent**, you've got the right one.

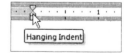

4. After dragging that triangular piece to the right, this is how it should look.

5. Done.

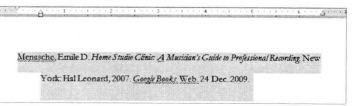

chapter 11

APA DOCUMENTATION

He is wise who knows the sources of knowledge—who knows who has written and where it is to be found.
> ~ A. A. Hodge

When do you need to use APA rather than MLA?

Put simply: When your professor tells you to. Most paper assignments that require research will tell you which documentation format to use. In English, it's almost always MLA. In the social sciences (psychology, sociology, and anthropology), it's APA (American Psychological Association). Other disciplines, such as business, criminology, nursing, linguistics, and economics also tend to use APA. When in doubt, of course, ask your professor.

When do you need to document? And when do you *not* need to document?

You need to document your source any time you use an idea or piece of information that is not yours. **Important:** This remains true even when you put the information in your own words. If you don't document your sources properly, you may be accused of plagiarism (see Chapter 7).

You don't need to cite "common knowledge," which includes strictly factual information that can be found in a number of different sources.

As with MLA, documentation in APA is a two-step process.

Just as you do with an MLA citation, you provide a brief citation within your paper (in parentheses) and a complete citation on the "reference list" page (we called this a "works-cited page" in MLA). There are other similarities between the two systems, but many, many small differences.

Why don't articles in APA journals look like my paper?

The main difference here is in line spacing. You're supposed to double-space, but articles that you see in published journals are generally single-spaced. There may be other slight differences as well. Bear in mind that the authors of those published articles had to submit their work to those journals in exactly the same format as what your professors expect from you.

APA Documentation Directory

IN-TEXT CITATIONS

When I say "in-text," I mean *your* text, the paper you're writing. For the examples here, pretend that these are sentences you would write in your paper. Pay attention to punctuation, spacing, and formatting.

In the social sciences, great value is placed on how recent the research is; as a result, the in-text citation will always include the year of publication.

Basic format

Most of the time, your citation will look something like this:

> **Participants in online communities can be separated into two groups: disclosers and listeners (Crawford, 2009).**

Author last name   Year of publication

If you want to name the source in the sentence, use a signal phrase:

SIGNAL PHRASE

> **According to Crawford (2009), participants in online communities can be separated into two groups: disclosers and listeners.**

SIGNAL PHRASE

A signal phrase is a brief reference to your source within your sentence; we call it this because it *signals* the source for your reader.

Papers written in APA format generally rely more on paraphrase and summary than quotation, but you will occasionally want to quote a source. When you do, you should include the page number in your citation:

> **As Crawford (2009) observed, "Listening is not a common metaphor for online activity" (p. 526).**

The above example, which uses a signal phrase to introduce the author, is the preferred method; if you don't use a signal phrase, it should look like this:

> **As one researcher has observed, "Listening is not a common metaphor for online activity" (Crawford, 2009, p. 526).**

Important: No matter how you identify the "source" (usually the author), it must correspond with a reference list entry; in other words, you must have a reference list entry that begins **Crawford.**

Verb tenses

Note that when using a signal phrase you should use past tense or present perfect tense: *Crawford found*, or *Crawford has found*. Again, this is in contrast to MLA guidelines, which call for almost all references to be in present tense.

Two authors

Use the ampersand (&) between names.

> **In contrast to their older counterparts, young adults tend to be more careful in managing their online identities (Madden & Smith, 2010).**

HOWEVER: If you refer to the authors in a signal phrase, use the word *and* rather than the ampersand:

> **According to Madden and Smith (2010), young adults tend to be more careful in managing their online identities than their older counterparts.**

Three to five authors

Note the use of the ampersand (&) and the placement of commas.

> **Since 2006, the number of teen bloggers has dropped by 50% (Lenhard, Purcell, Smith, & Zickuhr, 2010).**

HOWEVER: If you refer to the authors in a signal phrase, use the word *and* rather than the ampersand:

> **According to Lenhard, Purcell, Smith, and Zickuhr (2010), the number of teen bloggers has dropped by 50% since 2006.**

If you refer to the same source again in the same paragraph:

> **Older adults, however, have continued to blog at approximately the same pace (Lenhard et al.).**

If you refer to the same source again later in the paper (but not in the same paragraph):

> **Overall, nearly half of adults in 2010 were using social networking sites, a 27% increase from 2006 (Lenhard et al., 2010).**

Six or more authors

You'll need to name all the authors on the reference list page at the end of your paper, but you don't need to do so here; simply list the first author and *et al.*, followed by the year.

> Social media sites such as blogs, photo-sharing sites, Wikis, and similar sites are estimated to be responsible for one third of all new Internet content (Finin et al., 2008).

> OR:

> According to Finin et al. (2008), social media sites such as blogs, photo-sharing sites, Wikis, and similar sites are estimated to be responsible for one third of all new Internet content.

No author listed / author unknown

This will happen most commonly when you're citing a reference work, such as an encyclopedia, that doesn't name individual authors of articles. Use the entire title of the source if it is short; if it's longer, use a shortened form. The following example is from an *Encyclopædia Britannica* article about Twitter:

> The site has also been effectively used to raise money for a variety of causes; after the Haiti earthquake in 2010, Twitter users helped the Red Cross raise more than $8 million in just two days ("Twitter" 2012).

Note: How you abbreviate the title is up to you, but be sure to use the first word (unless it's *a, an* or *the*)—because this is the word a reader would be looking for on the reference list page.

Citing two or more works at the same time

If more than one source has made a similar (or identical) observation, cite all the sources. This adds to the reader's perception of you as a thorough researcher.

Here's an example from the article by Kate Crawford I used on page 189:

> "Speaking up" has become the dominant metaphor for participation in online spaces such as blogs, wikis, news sites and discussion lists (Karaganis, 2007; Bruns, 2008).

A source within a source

In other words, imagine that you're reading an article by Crawford; in the article, Crawford uses Nick Couldry as a source, and you want to make reference to Couldry's idea. First, use a signal phrase to name the author (Couldry, in this case) whose idea you're using; then, in a parenthetical reference, provide the information about the source where you read Couldry's idea.

> **Nick Couldry cited reciprocity and embodiment as two distinct advantages of aurality (as cited in Crawford, 2009).**

Note: Your reference list should have an entry for Crawford, not Couldry.

Sources without page numbers

Many non-print sources will not have page numbers; some will include paragraph numbers, and if they do, you should include this information after the date:

> **In contrast to the older counterparts, young adults tend to be more careful in managing their online identities (Madden & Smith, 2010, para. 4).**

If the paragraphs aren't numbered, use section headings:

> **In 2008, a teenager in Ohio committed suicide after a nude photo she had sent her boyfriend was forwarded to many other students at her high school (Common Sense Media, 2010, Why sexting matters).**

Organization or group as author

If your source doesn't list a specific person as an author, you should use this guideline. The first time you cite the source, use the entire organization name; if you cite it again, use an abbreviation. If you only cite it once, don't include the abbreviation.

First reference: (**Common Sense Media [CSM], 2010**)

Additional references: (**CSM, 2010**)

Long quotation (also known as block quotation)

If you quote something that is 40 words or longer, format it as follows.

Your writing, to introduce the quotation.

While others describe lurkers as passive, Kate Crawford (2009) examined their behavior from a different perspective:

Block quotation, indented 1/2 inch from left. The right margin stays the same. It's double-spaced just like the rest of your text.

Listening has not been given sufficient consideration as a significant practice of intimacy, connection, obligation and participation online; instead, it has often been considered as contributing little value to online communities, if not acting as an active drain on their growth. (p. 527)

Your writing, to comment on the quotation.

This reconceptualizing of lurking leads to new ways of thinking about what it means to participate in an online community.

Also note that the block quotation ends with the page number where you found the quotation, inside parentheses and *after* the punctuation mark.

Formatting note: To see how to create a block quotation in Microsoft Word, see page 161.

Personal communication

If you interviewed someone or communicated with a source via email, telephone, or other electronic means, use the person's first initial and last name, along with the words *personal communication* in your citation. This guideline also applies to personal letters. Note: You do not need a reference list entry for these sources.

According to J. Mino (personal communication, August 18, 2012), the rules for psychological experiments using college students as subjects have changed dramatically over the last twenty years.

REFERENCE LIST ENTRIES

FIRST, SOME UNIVERSAL GUIDELINES

Capitalization of book and article titles

Yet again, APA has very different rules from MLA. This is easier.

Always capitalize	the first word of the title
	the first word of a subtitle
	proper nouns (names, monuments, etc.)
Do *not* capitalize	anything else

Examples:

Reputation management and social media

Following you: Disciplines of listening in social media

Media, celebrities, and social influence: Identification with Elvis Presley

Capitalization of journal names

Always capitalize	first and last words; all the important words
Do *not* capitalize	prepositions, articles (unless they start the title)

Examples:

Abnormal Psychology

Journal of Medical Internet Research

The International Journal for the Psychology of Religion

Italics: needed vs. not needed

Always italicize	journal titles (see previous examples)
	volume numbers (but NOT issue numbers) of journals
Do *not* italicize	anything else, including book titles (unlike MLA!); note: there are some rare cases where a book title will need to be italicized (see pages 198-199).

Quotation marks: needed vs. not needed

You will never need to use quotation marks on your reference list page; of course, you may need them in the text of your paper.

Author names: one, two, or many

Always begin with the author's last name, followed by initial(s) for first name and middle name (if available). If you use two initials, type a space after the period following the first initial. Use an ampersand (&) rather than the word *and* before the final name. When you have multiple authors, you list all of them last-name-first:

> **One author**: Smith, D. G.
>
> **Two authors**: Smith, D. G., & Philips, J. T.
>
> **Three to seven authors**: Smith, D. G., Philips, J., & McBride, B. Q.
>
> **Eight or more authors**: List the first six authors as you usually would, then tpe an ellipses (three periods, with spaces between each), and then the final author name:
>
> > Smith, D. G., Philips, J., McBride, B. Q., Walcott, T., Diaby, A., Oxlade-Chamberlain, A., . . . Vermaelen, T.

Abbreviations of months

Unlike MLA, APA does not abbreviate months; write them all out.

Abbreviations of publishers' names

If the publisher is listed as, for example, The Macmillan Company, you would simply write Macmillan. However, keep the words *Press, Association,* and *Books* when they are part of the publisher name, e.g., University of Chicago Press.

Abbreviations of states

When you write the city and state of publication, use the two-letter postal abbreviations for states names: MA, NY, CA, etc. Look up *state postal abbreviations* online if you're not sure.

Spaces

With some of the examples on the following pages, it's hard to tell where you should have a space. You always have a space after any mark of punctuation (comma, period, colon, semi-colon); also rememember that between each "part" of an entry (like, for example, between a magazine name and its date of publication), you always need a space.

Hanging indent

Reference list entries should use a hanging indent—see page 179 for how to format this.

Lengthy URL addresses

Particularly when you're using a database, you'll find some very long URL addresses. Some guidebooks to APA say not to include the URL in this case, mainly because it won't work (for most databases, you have to log in first, so the URL won't take you to the article itself). But also, who would retype it all anyway when it's easier to simply put in a couple of search terms from the article's title? Still, many professors will want to see *something* at the end of your entry (assuming there's no DOI available), so it's probably better to have something than nothing.

Two alternatives:

- Include the URL for the database itself, which you would find by searching for it online. Here's one for a database (Academic OneFile) many students use: http://www.gale.cengage.com/PeriodicalSolutions/academicOnefile.htm.
- Find the article online and use that URL.

Citation generators

In most databases, you'll find a "citation generator," a tool that will give you a reference entry for the source you're using. You choose the documentation system (MLA, APA, etc.), tell the software how to export the information, and then copy and paste it into your paper. This can be a great tool, but be aware that the results are not always entirely correct. Check the entry against the guidelines here and use common sense. The next page shows how to use a citation generator in Academic OneFile, a popular database.

Using a citation generator

If you use a library database for research, you'll find that many of the databases offer a "citation generator." This can save you some time if you have a number of database sources, but be sure to check the entries—they often have mistakes.

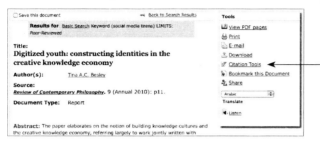

In many databases, you'll find a box of tools like this one. Click on **Citation Tools**.

I recommend using the Save function (the "third party software" option is complicated). Make sure you switch it to **APA**.

You'll then have the option to open it (in a program you choose) or save it.

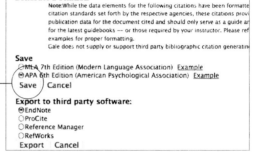

If you save it, you then need to find the file and open it; it will open in a web browser screen; from there, copy and paste the entry to your word processing program. You'll need to fix some of the formatting (spacing, hanging indent, etc.).

If you decide to open it, choose the program you're using to write your paper in, e.g., Microsoft Word. This should give you a properly formatted citation; the one below is almost perfect, except that they should have capitalized the first word of the subtitle.

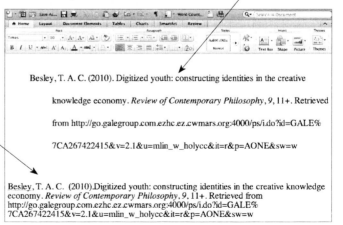

BOOKS

Note: For a detailed explanation of where to find specific information (publisher, city of publication, etc.) on the cover, spine, and inside the first few pages of a book, see MLA chapter, pages 154-55.

Book with one author

> Author's Last Name, Initials. (Year of publication). *Book title: Book subtitle**. City of Publication, State Abbreviation: Publisher.

* Include subtitle after a colon, and always capitalize the first word after the colon.

> Pollan, M. (2006). *The omnivore's dilemma: A natural history of four meals*. New York, NY: Penguin.

Book with an editor

The editor is listed as the "main" author for the sake of the reference list entry. Keep in mind, though, that if you cite particular articles from within this book, you need an entry for each of these authors too. Yes, this is a little confusing. See next entry for how to cite a specific article (or two) from a book with an editor.

> Noor Al-Deen, H. S. & Hendricks, J. A. (Eds.). (2012). Social media: Usage and impact. Lanham, MD: Lexington Books.

Note: If there is only one editor, the abbreviation would be (**Ed.**).

Part of a book with an editor / article or essay in an anthology

If you found an article in a book that has other articles by different authors, this is how you document the article you're using.

The following book was edited (all the articles were selected by the editors) by Hana S. Noor Al-Deen and John Allen Hendricks. I want to cite one of the articles in the book; it's about Twitter in college classrooms, by Alec R. Hosterman. Start by naming the author of the article; then, give the year of publication and the article title. *Then*, cite the editor and name of the book, starting with the word *In*, followed by page range of article.

> Hosterman, A. R. (2012). Tweeting 101: Twitter and the college
> classroom. In H. S. Noor Al-Deen & J. A. Hendricks (Eds.), *Social*
> *media: Usage and impact* (pp. 93-110). Lanham, MD: Lexington
> Books.

Note: This is one of those rare cases where you *do* italicize the book title.

Two or more books by same author

Unlike MLA, you don't need to do anything differently here. Simply cite each book completely.

Book that lists an edition

Many books (textbooks, especially) are republished with the same title but new content. If your book has an edition listed, it will probably be noticeable on the cover and/or the spine. In the reference list entry, put the edition after the title.

> Briggs, A., & Burke, P. (2010). *Social history of the media: From*
> *Gutenberg to the internet* (3rd ed.). Malden, MA: Polity.

Book(s) in more than one volume

If the book you're using is part of a number of volumes, your citation should specify this.

> Castells, M. (2009). **The rise of the network society: The information**
> **age: Economy, society and culture** (Vol. 2). Malden, MA: Wiley-
> Blackwell.

Book with no author

Don't write Anonymous or Anon. for the author. Just go straight to the title.

> *Primary Colors: A Novel of Politics.* (2006). New York, NY: Random
> House.

Book by an organization or group

Start with the name of the organization or group, followed by the date, and then book title.

> American Psychological Association. (2009). *Publication manual of the American Psychological Association,* (6th ed.). Washington, DC: American Psychological Association.

Book that has been translated

Start with the person who wrote the book, *not* the translator.

> Barthes, R. (1979). *The Eiffel Tower and other mythologies* (R. Howard, Trans.) New York, NY: Noonday.

Encyclopedia or dictionary

In most reference books (such as encyclopedias and dictionaries), no author is listed, so you simply start with the title of the entry. If there is an author, start with his or her name, of course.

> Botox. (2003). In *The new encyclopædia Britannica* (15th ed., vol. 2, p. 233). Chicago, IL: Encyclopedia Britannica.

PERIODICALS (Magazines, Newspapers, Journals)

Basic format

> Author last name, Initials. (Year). Title of article. *Title of Periodical, volume number*(issue number), pages. doi: OR Retrieved from URL.

- Journal articles will often include a "DOI," or digital object identifier. If you can find this, include it at the end of the entry as shown above.
- If you can't find a DOI, write *Retrieved from* and paste the URL (website address).
- Note how the journal's volume and issue are written: volume *23* is italicized, but the issue number (4) and its parentheses are not.

IMPORTANT: My guidelines here operate on the assumption that you will find these sources electronically rather than in print. As a result, if you do happen to use these sources in print (from an actual scholarly journal, magazine, or newspaper), you simply don't include the additional electronic information such as DOI or URL.

Paginated by volume or issue?

This is confusing. I'll illustrate with an example: a journal that has been publishing since, say, 1913 is now on volume 100. The first issue of this year would be called volume 100 issue 1; the second issue would be volume 100 issue 2; and so on. The first page of volume 1 will be, of course, page 1. Let's say that issue 1 is 322 pages. If issue 2 starts on page 323 (as most journals in psychology, sociology and anthropology do), then we would say that this journal is *paginated by volume*. If, on the other hand, volume 2 starts again at page 1, then we would say that it is *paginated by issue.*

Does it really matter? Not much, actually. As you'll see on the next two pages, the reference list entries end up being more or less identical either way. The APA says that you don't include the issue number if the journal is paginated by volume, but since it's often hard to tell how a journal is paginated, I would advise using the guideline for *article in a journal paginated by issue* in almost all cases (unless you're absolutely certain it paginates by volume).

Article in a journal paginated by volume

Note that the journal title and volume number (23) are italicized, but nothing else.

Crawford, K. (2009). Following you: Disciplines of listening in social media. *Continuum: Journal of Media & Cultural Studies, 23*, 525–535. doi: 10.1080/10304310903003270

Following you: Disciplines of listening in social media

Kate Crawford*

Media and Communications, University of Sydney, Sydney, Australia

This paper develops the concept of listening as a metaphor for paying attention online. Pejorative terms such as 'lurking' have failed to capture much detail about the experience of presence online. Instead, much online media research has focused on 'having a voice', be it in blogs, wikis, social media, or discussion lists. The metaphor of listening can offer a productive way to analyse the forms of online engagement that have previously been overlooked, while also allowing a deeper consideration of the emerging disciplines of online attention. Social media are the focus of this paper, and in particular, how these platforms are changing the configurations of the ideal listening subject. Three modes of online listening are discussed: background listening, reciprocal listening, and delegated listening; Twitter provides a case study for how these modes are experienced and performed by individuals, politicians and corporations.

Introduction

In his book on attention and modern culture, *Suspensions of Perception*, Jonathan Crary reminds us that 'the ways in which we intently listen to, look at, or concentrate on anything have a deeply historical character' (1999, 1). He observes that the ways in which we pay attention – and what we pay attention to – shift over the centuries, as part of a larger shaping of subjectivity. Along with new technological forms of display, communication, recording and playback come new forms of looking, listening and interacting; they afford new ways of focusing as well as defocusing attention. In doing so, they also become part of the ongoing reconstruction of the limits of human capacities. They contribute to the sense of what is possible, as well as to the qualities of being.

My aim here is to engage with a set of emerging modes of paying attention online, and to propose that they be considered practices of listening. As a metaphor, listening is useful; it captures some of the characteristics of the ongoing processes of receptivity that mark much online engagement. Nick Couldry argues that aural terms are more able 'to register media's social presence' as they have distinct 'advantages as a source of metaphors for thinking about the social world' (2006, 6). He writes of the 'reciprocal, embodied nature of listening; its embeddedness always in an intersubjective space of perception' (6). This intersubjectivity is important to the functioning of many online spaces. It is my hope that the concept of listening will allow us to analyse the various affordances of online attention, and to assess the ways in which we listen also shape us as late modern subjects.

Listening online could be considered in any number of contexts: be it wikis, MUDs, blogs, mailing lists, and even RSS feeds. For my purposes here, I am taking the example of social media, and Twitter in particular, as spaces where we can observe various types of

*Email: k.crawford@unsw.edu.au

ISSN 1030-4312 print/ISSN 1469-3666 online
© 2009 Taylor & Francis
DOI: 10.1080/10304310903003270
http://www.informaworld.com

Article in a journal paginated by issue

Note that the journal title and volume number (23) are italicized, but nothing else.

Greitemeyer, T., & Osswald, S. (2011). Playing prosocial video games
increases the accessibility of prosocial thoughts. *The Journal Of Social
Psychology, 151*(2), 121-128. doi:10.1080/00224540903365588

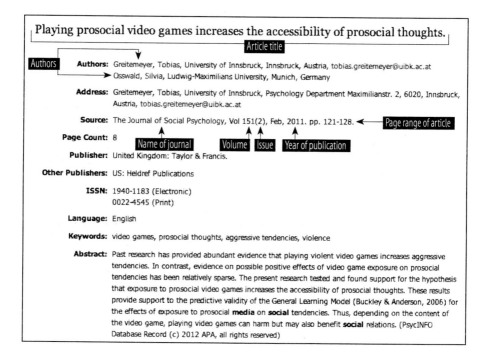

Scroll down to the bottom of the screen to find the DOI information.

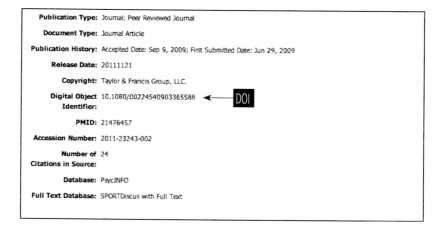

Article in a journal with no DOI

Follow the two previous guidelines, but instead of a DOI, provide the URL for the website where you found the article.

> **Steele, J. R. & Brown, J. D. (1995). Adolescent room culture:**
> **Studying media in the context of everyday life. *Journal of Youth***
> ***and Adolescence, 24*(5), 551-576. Retrieved from http://www.**
> **springerlink.com/content/m4m7669383042241/**

Article in a magazine (found online)

Note the differences between this page and the facing page. Exact same article, but two very different ways of documenting it. The online version, on this page, has no information about volume, issue, or page range, and it's not clear whether the article is from *The Daily Beast* (an online-only magazine) or *Newsweek*. I went with *The Daily Beast* in my citation because that name is more prominent on the page, and in the URL. **About the URL:** Note that with online magazines, you only include the homepage URL, not the entire address.

> Begley, S., & Interlandi, J. (2008, May 24). The dumbest generation? Don't be dumb. *The Daily Beast*. Retrieved August 4, 2012 from http://www. thedailybeast.com

Article in a magazine (found in database)

This version of the article, in contrast to what you see on the previous page, contains all of the information you *should* have in an APA reference entry. In other words, you're better off using the databases to find articles—or at least going to the database to look for an article that you've found online in order to get complete citation information. (It makes your research look more scholarly.)

About the URL: Just use the homepage of the URL rather than the entire address.

Begley, S., & Interlandi, J. (2008, June 2). The dumbest generation? Don't be
  dumb. *Newsweek, 151*(22), 42. Retrieved from http://go.galegroup.com

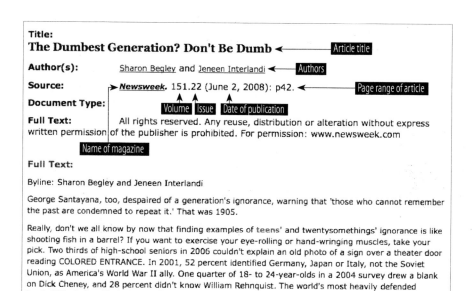

Article in a newspaper

This is very similar to the entry for a magazine article. However, unlike reference entries for magazine articles, with newspaper articles I recommend that you search for them online, through the newspaper's website, rather than through a database. If you do find a newspaper article in a database, try to also find the online version so that you can include a URL. Note that with online newspaper articles, you only include the homepage URL, not the entire address.

Ahles, A. (2012, April 4). Young woman gives social-media voice to Travelocity's gnome. *Seattle Times*. Retrieved August 4, 2012 from http://seattletimes. nwsource.com

Editorial in a newspaper

An editorial is an opinion essay written by the editors of a newspaper. Typically, it does not include author names (because it's written by the editorial board, a group of four to ten editors). This means that your reference list entry will start with the title of the editorial rather than author name(s); add the word editorial as shown below. Note that with online newspaper articles or editorials, you only include the homepage URL, not the entire address.

For a letter to the editor, start with the name of the letter writer, as author, and instead of the word *editorial* inside the brackets, write *Letter to the editor* (no italics).

The few, the proud, the women [Editorial]. (2012, July 13). *The New York Times*, p. A16. Retrieved August 8, 2012 from http://www.nytimes.com

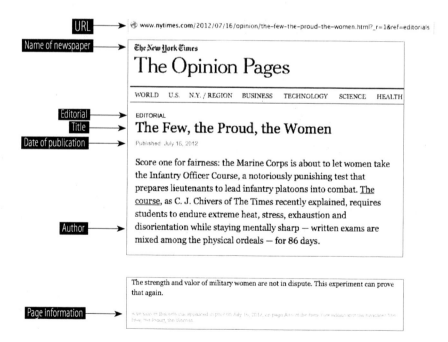

OTHER SOURCES, NON-PERIODICAL

Note: I have included only a few of the most common types of non-periodical sources. For more complete coverage, please see The Owl at Purdue's online APA guidelines (Google: Owl Purdue APA).

Online page published by group or organization

American Psychological Association. (2010). Managing your stress in tough economic times. *American Psychological Association.* Retrieved August 8, 2012 from http://www.apa.org/helpcenter/economic-stress.aspx

• With many websites produced by an organization, the name of the organization itself can be listed as the author. Obviously, if there's a person's name listed as the author, use it.

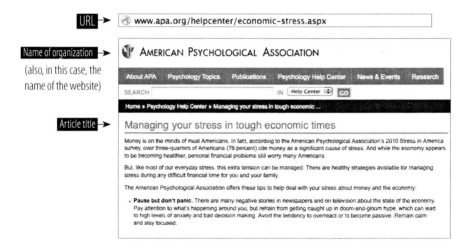

Email message

Do not include a reference entry for an email message or any other kind of personal communication. Instead, cite it within your paper according to the guideline on page 187.

Online video and/or television series

I chose this video for two reasons: first, because it's typical of the kind of video resource you might find online, and second, because it presented a real challenge in terms of finding some necessary information about writers and producers.

> Rushkoff, D. & Dretzin, R (Writers) & Dretzin, R. (Producer). (2010). *Digital nation: Life on the virtual frontier* [Video file]. Retrieved August 8, 2012 from http://www.pbs.org/wgbh/pages/frontline/digitalnation/

Even after watching some of the video, I couldn't find the names of the writers or producers. I looked around the page more, and that's when I found Credits, which gave me the information I needed.

Note: Some APA experts might advise you to treat this as a film or a television series. For these guidelines, please refer to a site such as the OWL at Purdue for more information.

SAMPLE APA PAPER

Over the next ten pages, you can see all elements of an APA-formatted paper. **Everything, everywhere, is double-spaced.**

Title page

1 Running head: TECHNOLOGY AND AUTISM   1

Page number, aligned with
right-hand margin (1 inch in)

Technology and Autism:

How Technology Is Helping Children with Autism

Communicate   Title:

Jesse J. Sands   Title Part Two

Holyoke Community College   Your Name

Your College

2 Author Note

This paper was prepared on 14 October 2015 for English

101, Section 32, taught by Professor Cooksey.

1 Yes, it really should say Running head (but only on the title page), followed by a colon and the first part of your paper title in all caps.

2 The author note provides specific information about the course for which you're submitting the paper.

Abstract page

From this page to the end of your reference page, your running header will appear at the top left of every page in caps. The running header is a shortened form of your title, and it should use the first words of the title, not a subtitle.

TECHNOLOGY AND AUTISM   2

Abstract

Modern technology is becoming an ever more dominant force in everyone's lives. One form of modern technology, the touchscreen tablet, may offer some beneficial solutions to autistic children who have communication deficits. This paper will examine the ways in which touchscreen tablets (along with their software applications) may be aiding children with varying degrees of autism spectrum disorder.

First and subsequent pages

Even though you have a title page, APA Style says that you repeat the title here. Center it, but don't put quotation marks around it or italicize (unless you're referencing an article or book within your title; see page 188).

TECHNOLOGY AND AUTISM   3

Technology and Autism:

How Technology Is Helping Children with Autism Communicate

Most would agree that modern technology is affecting the daily lives of every person to some extent. The beneficial impact of today's technology—computers, social media sites, smartphones, and tablets—is up for debate, but, whether or not you embrace technology, the reality is that millions of people every day are turning to their smart technologies as a means to stay connected and communicate. These modern technologies may hold new enabling potentials and growth capabilities for one group in particular: children with autism (Mozes, 2013). Although it has long been known that children with autism have difficulty communicating and expressing their emotions, the evidence to support technology being helpful to this group has only recently been explored. However, the limited research done may indicate a more productive future for those afflicted with autism.

Autism Spectrum Disorder (ASD) is a complex neuro-developmental disorder that affects one in sixty-eight children (American Psychiatric Association [APA], 2015). Because autism is a

* Note: My margins here are not to scale—make sure you use 1-inch margins.

TECHNOLOGY AND AUTISM   4

neurological disorder, it affects the functioning of the brain, resulting in difficulty using and understanding language, trouble relating to people, and repetitive body movements. Autism's symptoms and their severity vary greatly from person to person (Centers for Disease Control and Prevention [CDC], 2015); however, the group that would seem to benefit most from using technology are those who have trouble with communication. Some children diagnosed with autism are extremely limited in their ability to communicate, to the extent that some in this class are completely nonverbal. Many of these nonverbal children are completely unable to express their needs, desires, and inner emotions due to their lack of ability to use words. If a nonverbal child is experiencing distress—physical, mental, or emotional—and is incapable of outwardly expressing it using words, deficits in learning and communication skills will often result (CDC, 2015).

Certainly, the technology that seems to hold the most potential for empowering children with ASD is the touchscreen tablet, e.g. the iPad, equipped with appropriate software. At first, children with ASD were drawn to these devices because of their mobility, simple design, and ease of use (Seshadri, 2012). These simple characteristics are the very traits that make touchscreen tablets more useful to children with

TECHNOLOGY AND AUTISM   5

limited communication ability. Vicki Clarke, a Speech Language
Pathologist and Augmentative Communication Specialist, has argued
that software with simple and predictable behavior is beneficial to
children with ASD because it is "easy to understand and comforting"
(as cited in Woollaston, 2014). In reference to her clients, speech and
language therapist Rhiannan Walton has said, "Technology responds
in the same way every time; you press a button and it responds how
you expect it to" (as cited in Woollaston, 2014). These claims imply
that touchscreen tablet technology, with appropriate software, can help
bridge the gap in understanding and communication within this class.

In 2014 a study was published focusing on the ability of
touchscreen tablets to aid in vocabulary and communication skills
development in children with ASD (Ganz, Boles, Goodwyn, & Flores,
2014). The study consisted of three 8-to 14-year olds being shown
actions and nouns with an application called iCommunicate, and
then being prompted to describe what was happening after the video
had concluded. The results of the study show that the participants
"required less intrusive prompts over time." Furthermore, Ganz also
observed that the participants "demonstrated a significant increase
in their use of nouns and verbs," both during interventions and
spontaneously (Ganz, et al., 2014, p.10). The conclusion of this study
not only supports the idea that technology can aid in the development

TECHNOLOGY AND AUTISM 6

of communication skills, but it also provides socially relevant information because of the implication that children with ASD can become more independently verbal.

Accordingly, the use of technology to aid in the communication of children with severe communication disorders is known as augmentative and alternative communication, or AAC. Before the use of tablets was recognized as a means to aid communication within this group, limited options were available to parents and caretakers of children with ASD wishing to facilitate communication. The most widely used method of AAC comes in the format of cards with images on them, which nonverbal children could hand to a caretaker or point at to indicate a specific emotion or desire (Liat, 2013). Although simple and cheap, this method does not come without its restrictions; the cards can only display images, and the time it takes to find the desired card(s) often takes longer than the attention span of the child. Another option for providing AAC is using an expensive, bulky electronic device that offers audio and digital display. These devices can be customized to individual needs, but lack the portability and functionality of the average tablet computer.

However, the current array of touchscreen tablets are not only affordable and portable, they are extremely versatile in their application due to the rapidly expanding library of educational

TECHNOLOGY AND AUTISM   7

software. Parents of children diagnosed with ASD can now design
their own applications tailored to their child's specific needs and
learning styles (Seshadri, 2012). The application and website
Wonkido, created by Tricia Estrada, is designed to teach children
with ASD social and life skills. Inspired by her own son, Estrada saw
this as an opportunity to help her child as well as help many other
children with autism. In addition, the Strides program, a U.S. based
program that encourages language through equine therapy and speech-
generating devices, is utilizing iPads equipped with speech-generation
software designed to help children with ASD externalize what they are
experiencing internally (Clark, 2013). Founder of the Strides program,
Catherine Markosky, has said:

> We witnessed one child communicate his understanding of
> addition, and the parents were completely unaware that their
> child even knew his numbers. . . . That's the beauty of the project;
> discovering that there's a person in there just waiting to be heard.
> (Clark, 2013)

1

The potential of digital technology aiding autistic children with
communication deficits seems to be recognized by parents, caregivers,
and researchers alike. Although the hardware itself is becoming more

---

1   A long quotation (40 words or more) requires special formatting. Indent the entire
    quotation 1/2 inch (the same as a new paragraph). Don't use quotation marks.
    Retain double-spacing. Add citation at end, after the period.

TECHNOLOGY AND AUTISM . 8

affordable and portable, it's the software that is truly maximizing the capabilities of children with ASD. The software market will continue to grow as families and parents of children with ASD become more aware of the inherent possibilities digital technology offers. Current study and information is limited due to the somewhat recent concept of touchscreen tablets being used as a form of AAC, but with the continued development of educational software the research is sure to continue.

See next page for references.

References

Reference page

Indentation:
First line of each entry: 1 inch
Second (and additional) line(s): 1.5 inches
See *Formatting a hanging indent*, page 143.

Continue running header

Continue page numbers

TECHNOLOGY AND AUTISM   9

American Psychiatric Association. (2015). What is autism spectrum

disorder? *American Psychiatric Association*. Retrieved October 11,

2015 from http://www.psychiatry.org/patients-families/autism/what-

is-autism-spectrum-disorder

Centers for Disease Control and Prevention. (2015). Facts about ASD.

Centers for Disease Control and Prevention. Retrieved October 11,

2015 from http://www.cdc.gov/ncbddd/autism/facts.html

Centers for Disease Control and Prevention. (2015). Diagnostic criteria.

Centers for Disease Control and Prevention. Retrieved October 11,

2015 from http://www.cdc.gov/ncbddd/autism/hcp-dsm.html

Clark, L. (2013, November). Using an ipad to help nonverbal autistic

children speak. *Wired*. Retrieved October 11, 2015 from http://

www.wired.co.uk/news/archive/2013-11/18/autism-ipad-speech

Ganz, J.B., Boles, M.B., Goodwyn, F.D., & Flores, M.M. (2014). Efficacy

of handheld electronic visual supports to enhance vocabulary in

children with ASD. *Focus on Autism and Other Developmental

Disabilities, 29*(1), 3-12. doi: 10.1177/1088357613504991

Double-spacing

TECHNOLOGY AND AUTISM   10

Mozes, A. (2013, August 2). Smart technology may help kids with autism learn, communicate. *Health Day*. Retrieved October 11, 2015 from http://consumer.healthday.com/ cognitive-and-neurological-health-information-26/autism-news-51/smart-technology-may-help-kids-with-autism-learn-communicate-678876.html

Seshadri, S. (2012, May 15). Ipad gives voice to kids with autism. *CNN*. Retrieved October 11, 2015 from http://www.cnn.com/2012/05/14/tech/gaming-gadgets/ipad-autism

Woollaston, V. (2014, April 6). How ipads are helping children with autism: Tablets develop communication skills because they are 'predictable and neat.' *Daily Mail*. Retrieved October 11, 2015 from http://www.dailymail.co.uk/sciencetech/article-2594471/How-iPads-helping-children-autism-Tablets-develop-communication-skills-predictable-neat.html

Index